"A fresh and innovative addition to Hilton scholarship, this will be of particular interest to Christian educators, spiritual directors, and those who know the area in Nottinghamshire, England, where Hilton lived and worked. Bringing the medieval mystical tradition into dialogue with contemporary theology and spirituality, Fr. Kevin's analysis will surely encourage others to explore and to learn from Hilton's writings."

—Erica Kirk,
priest vicar, Southwell Minster, Nottinghamshire, England

"In a time of global anxiety, we need spiritual resources and practices as never before. *Mystic Bonfires* will be immensely valuable in guiding young people especially in the fourteenth-century mystical tradition, which is so practical and attractive in its theology of love. The book offers a unique introduction to the wisdom of Walter Hilton, who unlike many, wrote explicitly for ordinary Christians in their working lives."

—Alison Milbank,
University of Nottingham

"*Mystic Bonfires* revives Hilton's tradition to work in tandem with a creative and contemporary practical spiritual theology. Its integration of spiritual theology with pastoral theology points a way for pastors, spiritual directors, Christian educators, and church evangelists to recover this living contemplative tradition at the heart of the church's mission."

—Julia Gatta,
The University of the South

"Fr. Goodrich constructs a remarkable bridge between the spirituality of the High Middle Ages and contemporary Christianity. Although well-informed and critical, *Mystic Bonfires* is not primarily an academic study, although it would be a valuable resource in a variety of settings. . . . Fr. Goodrich presents a lucid and inspiring conversation across centuries of what Hilton would describe as 'reformation in faith and feeling.'"

—Richard Woods, OP,
Dominican University, emeritus

"The Christian tradition has treasure troves of practical wisdom, embodied spirituality, and moral reflection. Unfortunately, these treasures are obscured to many contemporary people who have become disillusioned by shallow substitutes and church salesmanship. Kevin Goodrich leads readers on a pilgrimage of recovery, discovering along the way a practical and spiritual theology designed for ordinary people. This book is for students, parents, professionals, tradespeople, and pensioners who long for a deeper life with God."

—JASON GABOURY,
author of *Wait with Me: Meeting God in Loneliness*

"Goodrich introduces and ignites a contemporary integration of spirituality, practical theology, and empirical studies, constructing a method for the growing enterprise of practical theology. Individuals and institutions enduring global and local crises can embrace such an approach and set the church, academy, and the most curious of society aflame by renewing and creating a liberative future. . . . This practical spiritual-theological method responds to social, cultural, and ecclesial problems and seeks a prophetic response of justice."

—SONJA B. WILLIAMS,
Eden Theological Seminary

"Packed with potential and possibilities, *Mystic Bonfires* sets forth a unique method for academia, the church, and laity to explore and incorporate mystic prayer practices in our modern context. It serves as a strong reminder of how much might yet be gleaned from early Christian theological pillars and mystics as we seek to integrate the active and contemplative life."

—GAIL BRECHT,
Christos Center for Spiritual Formation

Mystic Bonfires

Mystic Bonfires

*Walter Hilton and the Development of
Practical Spiritual Theology*

KEVIN GOODRICH, OP

Foreword by Bryan Froehle

WIPF & STOCK · Eugene, Oregon

MYSTIC BONFIRES
Walter Hilton and the Development of Practical Spiritual Theology

Copyright © 2022 Kevin Goodrich, OP. All rights reserved. Except for brief quotations in critical publications or reviews, no part of this book may be reproduced in any manner without prior written permission from the publisher. Write: Permissions, Wipf and Stock Publishers, 199 W. 8th Ave., Suite 3, Eugene, OR 97401.

Wipf & Stock
An Imprint of Wipf and Stock Publishers
199 W. 8th Ave., Suite 3
Eugene, OR 97401

www.wipfandstock.com

PAPERBACK ISBN: 978-1-6667-3186-6
HARDCOVER ISBN: 978-1-6667-2485-1
EBOOK ISBN: 978-1-6667-2486-8

JUNE 30, 2022 7:38 AM

To the three parish priests of my early years: Father William Persing, Mother Patricia Colenback, and Father Robert Duval. Without always knowing it, they helped kindle the fires of faith in a lively, and sometimes troublesome, boy and in an enthusiastic, if not sometimes overzealous, teenager. Each pastor inspired, nurtured, and cultivated my own sense of a call to the priesthood. For this, I am forever grateful.

"Be who God meant you to be and you will set the world on fire."
—St. Catherine of Siena

Contents

Foreword by BRYAN FROEHLE | vii

Introduction | ix

CHAPTER 1
Foundations of Practical Spiritual Theology | 1

CHAPTER 2
Walter Hilton: A Resource for
Practical Spiritual Theology | 24

CHAPTER 3
Hilton and Groome: A Dialogical Analysis | 43

CHAPTER 4
Hilton and Southwell Christians:
A Conversational Analysis | 64

CHAPTER 5
Possibilities of Practical Spiritual Theology | 81

APPENDIX I
Questions & Exercises | 97

APPENDIX II
Guidelines and Suggestions for Using the Method | 123

Bibliography | 133

Foreword

INTEREST IN SPIRITUALITY has grown dramatically over the past few decades. This has been the case across the various forms of religion, regions of the world, and people in general, from scholars and leaders to ordinary people. As the Church in the global north struggles with profound cultural shifts challenging its growth and even its future, and the Church in the global south continues to grow in vibrancy, the need for careful and creative attention to spirituality and spiritual formation is paramount.

The Church of the global north will require both creativity and continuity in its engagement with past faith and practices if it is to thrive in a post-secular age. It will require retrievals of historical spiritualities and the development of new Christian spiritualities in response to today's challenges. This is a particular challenge for those engaged in lay and ordained ministries, the practice of spiritual direction, and formation work. The Rev. Dr. Kevin Goodrich, O.P., a former doctoral student of mine, is at the forefront of this important interdisciplinary, scholarly, and pastoral work.

I first met Father Kevin when I was the director of the Ph.D. program at St. Thomas University in Miami, Florida. My first impressions were of a contemplative Christian, an Anglican Dominican, possessing a creative spirit that captures the attention of others through a strong personal presence whether in conversation, teaching, or preaching. His creative spirit was quickly evident in his ready combination of prayer, scholarship, and the practice of ministry. These personal gifts, honed through years of study and pastoral ministry in diverse settings, are revealed in this book. Though an Episcopal priest and spiritual director anchored in the Anglican tradition, Father Kevin has been formed in critical ways within Evangelical, Catholic, and Mainline Christian institutions. He has ministered in rural, suburban, and urban settings in Canada and the United States. He has supervised seminarians from varied denominational backgrounds in field education programs. He has traveled both sides of the Atlantic as an itinerant preacher, preaching at small faithful congregations and lively historic cathedrals. His teaching at Protestant and Catholic universities has enriched his abilities as a translator between Christian traditions and an advocate for what C.S. Lewis called "mere" Christianity. Fr. Kevin's breadth of experience with the Christian tradition is revealed in this book.

Mystic Bonfires: Walter Hilton and the Development of Practical Spiritual Theology will be useful to readers from a variety of Christian traditions. I particularly commend its use as a secondary textbook in advanced undergraduate courses, most especially for graduate courses in practical theology, pastoral theology and leadership, spiritual direction, and Christian formation and education. Practitioners in those fields will also benefit greatly from the book. His work informed my own thinking and will surely broaden that of students and practitioners as they seek to understand their own fields and provide resources for engaging in the work of Christian spirituality. While Rev. Dr. Goodrich's emphasis is on the Western Christian mystical tradition, his method of Practical Spiritual Theology as described in this book holds promise for many contexts.

The Christian mystical tradition has something to say to Christianity globally. This book offers a flexible way for professional scholars to approach the work of retrieval in fresh ways. It empowers ministry practitioners to complete their own projects of investigation into the mystics. Such projects will surely create mystical laboratories in their own ministry settings drawing upon the deep well of wisdom from our foremothers and forefathers in the faith. Goodrich's combination of concerns from practical theology and spiritual theology, promises to enrich each theological discipline and most importantly lead to transforming practice by individuals and institutions.

I am particularly struck by the synthesis of medieval spirituality and contemporary concerns in the concept Goodrich describes as conative mysticism. His work helps us preserve the best of the tradition while commending it to address contemporary challenges.

I remember going to the Episcopal Cathedral in Miami to hear Father Kevin preach for the first time. I took my seat in a pew toward the back. He did not know I was there. What I did know, however, was that the congregation was highly engaged during his homily. It turned out that this was also the congregation's first time to hear him. It was the early 8 o'clock Sunday Eucharist and the congregation was very quiet until, at the end of the liturgy, the dean of the cathedral assured congregants that Father Kevin

Foreword

would be returning to preach again and be part of the Cathedral's life as a priest-in-residence. The congregation applauded. This was most definitely not par for the course at 8 o'clock Eucharists, yet thoroughly merited by Father Kevin. I add my applause to this book and recommend it to you. May the fire witnessed by generations of mystics give light to your mind and warmth to your heart as you read these pages.

Bryan T. Froehle, Ph.D.
Professor and Director, Ph.D. in Practical Theology Program
Palm Beach Atlantic University
February 2022

Introduction

SPIRITUALITY IN GENERAL and historical figures of the Christian tradition, especially mystics, are of interest to a wide variety of audiences within the academy, church, and society at large. This book is theological in nature. It explores the relationship between spirituality, spiritual theology, and practical theology. Each of these fields has its own methods, methodology, and literature. Each is a formal academic discipline practiced by scholars in the academy. Scholars from other disciplines also study spiritual texts and experiences. For example, scholars of religion, literature, and psychology. These scholars and their work are often enriching resources for theological reflection and pastoral practice. Work in spirituality, spiritual theology, and practical theology is done not only by professional theologians, but by Christian educators, clergy, and spiritual directors. Spirituality, understood in a multiplicity of ways by multitudes of people, is an area of human inquiry and practice engaged by billions of human beings, Christian and non-Christian.

The turn to the spiritual, to meaning making, and to a religious sense of finding a connection to something beyond oneself is one of the distinguishing features of human life. This book explores this connection theologically, from the perspective of the Christian theological tradition, especially as found in the medieval mystical tradition. The fourteenth-century English mystic Walter Hilton serves as a case study for this exploration. Chapters one and two will be helpful to all readers. Seminary and spiritual direction students will be introduced to fields and ideas that relate to the everyday exercise of their ministries. Graduate and advanced undergraduate students will become familiar with theological approaches to religion and spirituality that may complement or contrast their own methodologies of study. They will also be introduced to a Christian mystic and spiritual writer, Walter Hilton. Lay ministers and Christian educators will not only learn

Introduction

about the formal fields that shape their work but will also find insights into their work.

Chapter three will be of value to scholars as well as students of Christian education and spiritual formation interested in the philosophical dimensions of their work. More broadly, chapter three will be of interest to those practitioners interested in integrating concepts and ideas from past Christian practice with present practice. Chapter four, which highlights the responses of contemporary Christians to a historical mystic, will be of interest to all readers. Those students and others interested in combining theological reflection with empirical research will also find chapter four useful. Chapter five explores the possibilities and pitfalls of *practical spiritual theology*—the method of theological and spiritual inquiry proposed in this book. The chapter includes suggestions for scholars, practitioners, and communities. Appendix I includes questions for each chapter intended for use in a university course. Appendix II includes a second set of questions and exercises that may be used independently or in conjunction with the first set of questions for students in preparation for various kinds of ministry, including pastoral ministry, Christian education, and spiritual direction. This appendix also includes projects that can be used by scholars and ministry practitioners in small groups, faith communities, and institutions.

Dominican friar and scholar, Jordan Aumann, wrote in the preface to his book, *Spiritual Theology*, "Consequently, the study of the theology of Christian perfection should proceed scientifically and systematically, although its aim is not to produce scholars but to form holy Christians." The intention of this book is to encourage and sharpen scholarship as well as the spiritual vitality of readers and the people they teach, serve, and love. As Walter Hilton, Julian of Norwich, and many other medieval writers taught, love is both the means and the end of the Christian spiritual life.

Chapter 1

Foundations of Practical Spiritual Theology

RETRIEVAL AS INHERENT TO THE CHRISTIAN PROJECT AND CHRISTIAN SPIRITUALITY

Christianity claims that the historical is persuasive.[1] The faith meant to be lived today is rooted in the experience of the people of Israel, the centrality of the person of Jesus Christ, and in the witness of those who have followed Christ over the centuries. To be a Christian is to inherit a historical tradition, one that is living and continues to make claims upon the believer in the present. It is impossible to speak of either Christian spirituality or Christian living without referring to the past. This requires more than a passing reference. It necessitates a retrieval of the past for the purposes of the present.

Christian living today is enriched by engagement with the mystics and teachers of the spiritual life throughout the centuries. Mystics are those who have experienced the presence of God in their lives, often in unusual and remarkable ways. For the mystics, God was not a theoretical concept or known only through the words of the Bible. For the mystics, God was known experientially. God was known personally. God was not known or experienced completely, but God was encountered. Theologian and religious historian Bernard McGinn defines mysticism as "a special consciousness of the presence of God that by definition exceeds description

---

1. "Christianity, including its theology, is always looking back in order to move forward." Buschart and Eilers, *Theology as Retrieval*, 21.

and results in a transformation of the subject who receives it."[2] Theologian David Shaw recognizes that providing an exact definition for mysticism is difficult, but believes the definition for mystical theology provided by the *Oxford English Dictionary* is useful, "Mystical theology: belief in the possibility of union with or absorption into God by means of contemplation and self-surrender: belief in or devotion to the spiritual apprehension of truths inaccessible to the intellect."[3] Mysticism can also be defined as a human encounter with divine reality. Over the centuries Christian mystics have been spiritual guides for others seeking to experience the reality of God. There are varied approaches to studying the Christian mystics. The approach of this book is theological. Theological meaning is concerned with God. "Theology is any reflection on the ultimate concerns of life that point toward God."[4] Theology is the study of God.[5] This book suggests one way, among many, for not only studying the Christian mystics but for retrieving their wisdom to resource and inspire the spiritual lives of Christians today. The fourteenth-century English mystic, Walter Hilton, will serve as a case study to illustrate this theological method, which is called *practical spiritual theology*. A method that can be used in formal academic research by scholars, as well as informally by ministry practitioners, such as lay and ordained ministers, spiritual directors, and educators.

Theologians David Buschart and Kent Eilers use the term *retrieval* in the sense of "a mode or style of theological discernment that looks back in order to move forward."[6] This echoes the Second Vatican Council's call to "return to the sources."[7] It also includes what theologian John Webster describes as "an attitude of mind"[8] through which the "resources from the past are found distinctly advantageous for the present situation."[9] When contemplating the Christian mystics, including Walter Hilton, their writings are the primary point of entry into their lives and teachings. This concern with the written text is essential to the Christian life as manifested in Christianity's canonical traditions of Scripture. The canon is the official

---

2. McGinn, *The Flowering of Mysticism*, 26.
3. Shaw, *On Mysticism*, 2.
4. Grenz and Olson, *Who Needs Theology*, 13.
5. Grenz and Olson, *Who Needs Theology*, 29–33.
6. Buschart and Eilers, 21.
7. Vatican Council II, *Lumen Gentium*.
8. Webster, "Theologies of Retrieval," 584.
9. Webster, "Theologies of Retrieval," 584.

or authorized version of the Bible. Such canonical traditions look to the Old and New Testaments as the primary sources of the deposit of faith,[10] the content of the Gospel,[11] and the revelation of God.[12] In other words, Scripture forms the basic building blocks of Christianity, both as a belief system and as a way of life. The texts of the Old and New Testaments shape and support, in varying degrees, all expressions of Christianity spirituality.

Mystical writers do not supplant the Scriptures. Instead, they witness to the veracity of Scripture's claims, especially when it comes to the experience of God and in offering guidance for living a life that flows from this experience. They are witnesses, like bonfires on a dark winter's night, to the reality of God. Other human beings when questioning the reality of God in a dark world have been drawn by the warmth and witness of the mystics. This was often true in their lifetimes, such as when individuals sought spiritual counsel from the fourteenth-century English mystic, Julian of Norwich.[13] People sought her out because of her own experiences with God. Yet, the witness of many mystics, including Julian, have endured well past their lifetimes through their writings. Many who read Julian, a contemporary of Walter Hilton, continue to find themselves drawn toward God. Through her writings, readers find light to illuminate their own spiritual journeys in a sometimes cold and dark world. In the history of the Church, mystics have often been given an authoritative status as witnesses to God and as teachers of the spiritual life.

An authority rooted in the witness of their lives. An authority conferred by holiness. Holiness often means an unusual nearness to God. Holiness is moral strength and excellence in character and action.[14] The mystics are also witnesses in the sense given by Scripture. The author of Hebrews in the New Testament writes, "Therefore, since we are surrounded by so great

---

10. Rahner, *Karl Rahner*, 148. Rahner states, "What the church has once taken possession of as a portion of the revelation which has fallen to its share, as the object of its unconditional faith, is from then on its permanently valid possession. No doctrinal development could be merely the reflection of a general history of humanity . . . Yet, all human statements, even those in which faith expresses God's saving truths, are finite."

11. For a discussion on the content of the Gospel and the meaning of its symbols and texts, see Tracy, *Blessed Rage for Order*.

12. Like Rahner and Tracy, the theologian Richard Niebuhr acknowledges the givenness of revelation, but also its limits in being expressed within time by human beings. For more on this see Niebuhr, *The Meaning of Revelation*, 25–31.

13. Rolf, *Julian's Gospel*, 569.

14. Chan, *Spiritual Theology*, 88–89, 98.

a cloud of witnesses, let us also lay aside every weight and the sin that clings so closely, and let us run with perseverance the race that is set before us, looking to Jesus the pioneer and perfecter of our faith."[15] The mystics are part of the long line of human beings who have witnessed to the Christian way of being human. Christianity is more than a set of beliefs. It is a way of life.[16] A way of being alive in the fullest and most profound sense. The lives and words of mystics are an encouragement to those seeking to persevere in running the race of Christian living today. The concern of Christian mystical writers is the life of faith, especially the human encounter with the person of Jesus Christ. Their writings are classics, as they are an abiding fixture in Christian literature and offer an abundance of meaning for living the faith from the past to the present.[17] This book explores how classic texts, such as the writings of Walter Hilton, can resource and inspire the faith and practice of Christians today.[18] This work is interdisciplinary and of interest to scholars, lay and ordained ministers, spiritual directors, and educators.

The words *spiritual* and *spirituality* are often used in inexact ways. Typical of religion, defining spirituality can be quite elusive. Spirituality is often described as a short-hand reference for numinous experiences or those embodied values that guide one's life.[19] A numinous experience could be had when gazing at the stars, when waking from a dream, or having an unexpected realization about something. Sometimes spirituality is contrasted with religion. In this contrast, spirituality is a broader term for meaning making and spiritual practice for individuals. Religion in this comparison is a narrower term for the doctrines and institutions associated with organized religion.[20] While spiritualities of all kinds exist, this work focuses specifically on Christian spirituality. For some, the term *Christian spirituality* replaces the term *mysticism*.[21] For others, Christian spirituality

---

15. Heb 12:1–2 (New Revised Standard Version). All scripture from the NRSV unless otherwise noted.

16. McGrath, *Christian Spirituality*, 3.

17. Tracy, *The Analogical Imagination*, 154.

18. Classic texts have the potential to unjustly privilege certain voices while silencing others. Practical spiritual theology as a method asserts that mystical texts must be contextualized and critically engaged to mitigate some of these dangers.

19. Nassif et al., *Christian Spirituality: Four Views*, 12.

20. Religion and spirituality are not always tied together, not in formal terms. Spirituality manifesting as an alternative option to traditional religion is a reality. For more on this see Ammerman, *Sacred Stories, Spiritual Tribes*.

21. McGrath, *Christian Spirituality*, 5–6.

has a wider range of meanings, encompassing both the mystical experience and the entire experience of the Christian life.[22] This broader understanding offers more nuanced possibilities and greater theological clarity. Mystical writers, including Walter Hilton, encourage others to encounter the divine. Yet, these writers' recommendations are often more comprehensive than encountering God alone. For example, Hilton advises a man to attend faithfully to his business responsibilities and to his prayers.[23]

Historically, the formal study of the spiritual life has been done through the discipline of theology within the church and the university. In recent decades, however, a new academic discipline, *Christian Spirituality*, has emerged within academic theology.[24] This field is interdisciplinary, with scholars from a variety of fields examining the experiences of those seeking life in Christ. These multi-perspectival approaches are extremely helpful, enriching both academic and pastoral reflection on the subject. Pastoral approaches to spirituality are concerned with supporting Christians in practicing their faith.[25] For example, a group of Christians that meet regularly to deepen their practice of prayer are guided by a pastoral concern. While there are many ways of conceiving the academic discipline of Christian Spirituality, not all have explicitly pastoral ends. Thus, "spirituality as a discipline does not seek to deduce from revelation what Christian spirituality must be, or to prescribe theologically its shape, character, or functioning, or even necessarily to promote pastorally its exercise."[26] This book intends to bridge the academic with the pastoral. Walter Hilton, as well as other writers on the spiritual life, guided their readers to live their faith as fully as possible. Their work was explicitly theological. It was concerned with God. Their writings reflected the spiritual aspirations of specific people in specific situations. Their work was explicitly pastoral. This theological and pastoral primacy suggests that any examination of Hilton or other Christian mystics' writings must also be theological and pastoral in nature. This is especially essential when the goal of such an examination is to resource and inspire the spiritual lives of Christians today. Theologian Johannes van der Ven said, "Faith in God is the direct object . . . while God in and

---

22. Dreyer and Barrows, *Minding the Spirit*, xiii.
23. Jeffery, *Toward a Perfect Love*, 16.
24. Dreyer and Barrows, *Minding the Spirit*, 7.
25. Purves, *Pastoral Theology in the Classical Tradition*, 5.
26. Dreyer and Barrows, *Minding the Spirit*, 6.

through faith compromises the indirect object and hence the aim of... any kind of theological research whatsoever."[27]

SPIRITUAL THEOLOGY

In contrast to the newer academic discipline of Christian Spirituality, the older discipline of spiritual theology is always concerned with pastoral ends. Theologian Jordan Aumann notes that "Spiritual theology is that part of theology that, proceeding from the truths of divine revelation and the religious experience of individual persons, defines the nature of the supernatural life, formulates directives for its growth and development, and explains the process by which souls advance from the beginning of the spiritual life to its perfection."[28] Hilton was a spiritual director A guide to other Christians in pursuing the spiritual life. Hilton and others embraced direction as a part of their vocation, providing guidance to Christians directly, as well as offering guidance through the writing of letters and books.[29]

The writings of Walter Hilton, and many other mystics, are classic examples of spiritual theology. Hilton's chief aim is to encourage his readers at the beginning of the spiritual life, help them move toward the more advanced stages, and ultimately experience union with God.[30] This approach to spiritual counsel or spiritual direction was typical of many medieval mystics. The spiritual life was understood as a journey of growth. A

---

27. van der Ven, *Practical Theology*, 119.

28. Aumann, *Spiritual Theology*, 22.

29. Moral theology, the discipline of theological ethics often merges in the ordinary practice of providing guidance for lay and ordained ministers, spiritual directors, and educators. See Keating, *Spirituality and Moral Theology*.

30. Providing direction to individual Christians expressively for the purpose of guiding their spiritual development has a long tradition of practice within the Church. For example, see Demacopoulos, *Five Models of Spiritual Direction in the Early Church*. This has cognates with the modern spiritual direction movement, but also contrasts. For more on modern spiritual direction see Edwards, *Spiritual Director, Spiritual Companion*. In contrast, ancient and medieval directors were more directive in their counsel than modern directors, who are often influenced by therapeutic models of non-directive counseling and care. For most of Christian history, certainly in Hilton's time, directors did not undergo professional training and recognition in the manner of the modern spiritual director movement; rather, they became involved in this ministry because of their reputation for Christian maturity, as well as their record of effectively and pastorally guiding souls. Both professional and pastoral models of spiritual direction operate today. For further discussion of these issues see Bakke, *Holy Invitations: Exploring Spiritual Direction*.

journey with known stages, each with its own challenges and opportunities for growing closer to God. Perfection in the spiritual life was understood as union with God. Perfection was the end goal, inspired by Jesus' words to his followers to, "Be perfect as your heavenly Father is perfect."[31] Perfection as taught by Hilton and other mystics was a process. It was a journey. A quest. It involved character reformation, love toward neighbors, and the cultivation of the practice of prayer.

Theologian Simon Chan defines spiritual theology in a related way. He states, "Spiritual theology seeks to understand spiritual growth from beginning to end, making use of biblical and experiential data."[32] Chan describes systematic theology as an exploration of the rational concepts of Christian experience, while spiritual theology explores the experience behind those formulations.[33] In practice, it might be the difference between reading an essay on the theoretical aspects of building a fire and a how-to essay on building and enjoying a fire. Some divide spiritual theology into two subdisciplines, *ascetical theology* and *mystical theology*. Ascetical theology is concerned with growth in Christian virtues and living, whereas mystical theology is concerned with the specifics of the mystical experience and union with God. Sometimes ascetical theology is seen as being preliminary to mystical theology. Some writers use these terms interchangeably.[34] Hilton writes with both ascetical and mystical concerns.

Theologian Martin Thornton has a more expansive view of ascetical theology, defining it as "a practical and synthetic approach to all other branches of theology."[35] This more holistic view of spiritual or ascetical theology reflects the more integrated nature of theology in Hilton's time before the advent of the modern university. The modernization of university education has resulted in a variety of specializations and subdisciplines of theology.[36] Theology in the early Church meant, "the true, mystical knowledge of the one God."[37] Theology was done in partnership with prayer. Theology was ecclesial. It was done for and from within the Christian community. In the Middle Ages theology developed into a science in the "scholastic

---

31. Matt 5:48.
32. Chan, *Spiritual Theology*, 18.
33. Chan, *Spiritual Theology*, 16.
34. Dreyer and Burrows, *Minding the Spirit*, 28.
35. Chan, *Spiritual Theology*, 17.
36. Farley, *Theologia*, 34–44.
37. Farley, *Theologia*, 33.

sense of a method of demonstrating conclusions."[38] This began the separation of the study of theology from prayer and the pursuit of the Christian life. However, while early forms of the university developed in the Middle Ages, theology largely remained a discipline practiced and pursued within the structures established by the Church. At this time many teachers of the faith primarily understood theology as an exposition and study of Holy Scripture.[39] From Scripture, theologians would derive principles and truths to guide Christian living. While some laymen studied theology in the Middle Ages, it was principally the practice and profession of priests and other clergy. This clerical paradigm would later be questioned as adequate for doing theology in the modern world. However, the practice and training of clergy and now lay ministers remain important aspects of contemporary practical theology.

PRACTICAL THEOLOGY

Practical theology is a theological discipline encompassing the traditional arts of ministry as well as a broader academic discipline exploring the relationship between experience and faith.[40] Practical theology is concerned with practice—with what individual and Christian communities do. Theologian Don Browning describes the practical theological view as one that "goes from practice to theory and back to practice."[41] Practical theology can also be thought of as a reflection on human experience in conversation with the teachings, principles, and stories of the Christian faith. Practical theology as a modern academic discipline is often associated with the nineteenth-century pastor and theologian Friedrich Schleiermacher. Schleiermacher worked to secure theology's place in the university system of his time by defending its identity as a "positive science."[42]

This meant being able to articulate Christian claims and beliefs in a manner similar to other academic disciplines. A distinguishing feature of most modern academic disciplines is the critical dimension. Being critical

38. Farley, *Theologia*, 34.

39. Farley, *Theologia*, 37

40. This definition was used within the Ph.D. program in practical theology at St. Thomas University, Miami Gardens, Florida.

41. Browning, *A Fundamental Practical Theology*, 7.

42. Schleiermacher, *Brief Outline of Theology as a Field of Study*, xv. See also Farley, *Theologia*, 33.

not only in the sense of being able to judge theological claims as dubious in some cases but critical in being able to give attention to the presuppositions of theological claims. To question why a view is held, what influences a view, and a freedom to not only affirm a theological view, but to critique a view, even deconstruct a view.[43] Tied to this critical approach to theology is the need for theology to be able to express itself to many audiences, not just audiences within the Church. Theologian David Tracy expresses this perspective, which remains an important part of practical theology, "the need to develop . . . theology—available, in principle, to all intelligent, reasonable, and responsible persons."[44]

Traditional theology begins with the revealed truths of faith before moving to human experience.[45] Practical theology begins with human experience and then moves to the revealed truths of faith. In practice, all theory or theological constructs have some basis in experience (even if it has been rarified for centuries) and every action or experience is theory laden.[46] Behind any practice, whether prayer or pastoring, there are certain presuppositions. For example, the person praying assumes, even if they have not thought it through in any sophisticated way, that prayer is effective or may be effective. Practical theology through careful reflection and investigation seeks to make explicit the presuppositions behind practice.

For example, a minister may understand their vocation according to the theory, the theology, of their denomination. However, behind the stated theology, the theory, there is the influence of practice. The influence of centuries of pastors trying to live out the theological claims of their tradition in varied situations. Sometimes this influence on the theory or theology of pastoring is subtle, sometimes it is obvious, but in either case it is undeniable. Practical theology through careful reflection and investigation seeks to make explicit the presuppositions behind theory. There is no practice without theory, even if theory is only implicitly present in the mind of the practitioner and not consciously acknowledged. There is no theory without practice, even if the practice is only implicitly present in the mind of the theorist and not consciously acknowledged. Practical theology's critical

---

43. Tracey, *The Analogical Imagination*.
44. Tracy, *Blessed Rage for Order*, xiii.
45. Browning, *A Fundamental Practical Theology*, 5.
46. "Nearly all practical theologians today agree that there is no straight line from theory to practice." Cahalan and Mikoski, *Opening the Field of Practical Theology*, 2.

reflection on experiences and practices helps to define it in relation to other theological disciplines.

Practical theology orients one toward specific situations and contexts. Its purpose is not creating and applying universal systems of theology, thus "the aim of theology is not to work out a system that is enduring so much as to meet every day experiences with faith—and to express that faith in terms of everyday experience. Theology is an ongoing process."[47] Pastoral theology sometimes focuses on the work of the pastor in offering pastoral care and counsel. Sometimes pastoral theology focuses more broadly on the life of congregations. Sometimes it is understood to include topics related to the spiritual life and spiritual direction. This is because of the traditional role of priests and pastors as spiritual guides. Pastoral theology and spiritual theology often weave together in situations of pastoral counsel and spiritual direction. Pastoral theology is one subdiscipline of practical theology. Sometimes, in the British context, for example, the terms pastoral theology and practical theology are used synonymously.[48] What is crucial to understand about practical theology is its orientation toward experience and practice as being the first steps of theological reflection.

Practical theology is known for its use of the social sciences in doing theology. Practical theology utilizes both the methods and methodologies of these disciplines. For example, practical theologians sometimes use sociological surveys and interview groups as tools for gathering data for theological reflection.[49] They also sometimes use a sociological theory, such as a version of feminist or womanist theory, in analyzing a particular situation for theological reflection.[50] The practical theological method of starting with experience requires a "thick" description of the social setting being investigated. The setting could be a congregation, a classroom, or a spiritual direction session. This data gathering process is enhanced by using the insights and tools of academic disciplines, like sociology, dedicated to

---

47. Cahalan and Mikoski, *Opening the Field of Practical Theology*, 49.

48. Graham, *Transforming Practice*, 1–12. This understanding of practical or pastoral theology, while dominant in many circles, contrasts with other understandings of pastoral theology which seek to recapture a Christocentric and ecclesiological centered pastoral theology. See Purves, *Reconstructing Pastoral Theology*. This book engages with both understandings of pastoral theology, the latter understanding correlating with the aims of spiritual theology.

49. Swinton and Mowat, *Practical Theology and Qualitative Research*.

50. See Cahalan and Mikoksi, *Opening the Field of Practical Theology*; Mercer, "Feminist and Womanist Practical Theology."

descriptive and analytic work. Practical theologians are not social scientists, but they utilize the social sciences. In fact, practical theologians utilize any academic discipline, including the humanities and natural sciences, which enhances and assists their theological work.[51]

This willingness to partner with other academic disciplines gives practical theology a suppleness in theologizing about any topic, experience, or community. It is necessary for practical theologians to theologically critique their conversation partners from other disciplines so as not to naively adopt these other disciplines' philosophical assumptions which may conflict with certain Christian convictions. For example, Christian scholars and practitioners of pastoral care and counseling regularly critique and reformulate concepts found in psychology in light of their Christian convictions.[52] These are important considerations for Christian practitioners when they draw upon non-theological literature for help and insight for their work. The inverse of this is also true as stated by Clodovis Boff, "Theology must be able to uncover the properly 'christic' signification even where it is ideologically denied, as in certain historical movements in the practice of certain non-Christians."[53] Many Christian ministers, spiritual directors, and educators intuitively recognize the "christic" signification of insights from other fields and experiences for their work.

To retrieve the teachings of Walter Hilton and other mystics for the benefit of those living today, their writings must be brought into conversation with contemporary believers. This can be done theologically and sociologically through a comparative analysis between a mystic's ideas and that of contemporary thinkers. It can also be done empirically through interviews with contemporary believers. As part of its commitment to doing theology from below, practical theology sometimes makes use of sociological research methods, both qualitative and quantitative.[54] Quantitative research methods are often statistically demonstrable, rooted in theory, leading to number sets that can be compared and contrasted.[55] Qualitative research methods, such as structured interviews, provide feedback from

---

51. Cahalan and Mikoski state, "We also engage a wide range of nontheological disciplines, including psychology, sociology, cultural anthropology, performance studies, philosophy hermeneutics, history and economics." Cahalan and Mikoksi, *Opening the Field of Practical Theology*, 4.

52. Johnson, *Psychology & Christianity: Five Views*.

53. Boff, *Theology and Praxis*, 33.

54. van der Ven, *Practical Theology*, 80.

55. Creswell, *Research Design*, 29–30.

human subjects about their views and experiences and are often used to formulate theories. Both methods, especially the qualitative, can be useful in exploring how contemporary Christians respond or might respond to the writings of a mystic.

Practical theology, as a formal academic discipline, has more than one subdiscipline. One of special importance to the study of and practice of Christian spirituality is *Christian Education* or *Religious Education* also known as *Christian Formation* or *Spiritual Formation*.[56] The word formation has replaced education in some circles to emphasize the holistic nature of faith formation, especially in increasingly secular societies.[57] As Western societies move further away from grounding their cultural norms and values in a Judeo-Christian perspective, the more every person, including Christians, will be formed culturally in ways that are contrary to certain Christian values and ways of being in the world.[58] Christian belief and practice are to be shaped significantly by the love of God in Jesus Christ and not by other predominant cultural values. The mystics are a resource for anchoring contemporary faith and practice within the deep wells of the Christian faith. Mystics like Walter Hilton engaged in the work of spiritual formation. The current tendency to separate the work of clergy (pastoring and leadership),[59] spiritual directors (discernment and listening),[60] and

---

56. Miller-McLemore, *The Wiley-Blackwell Companion to Practical Theology*, 299. The term formation is particularly appropriate in discussions of spiritual theology and the concerns of writers like Hilton who understood the goals of the spiritual life to be transformational.

57. Root, *Faith Formation in a Secular Age*, x.

58. Hirsch, *The Forgotten Ways*, 106–116. Hirsh identifies my cultural challenges to Christian faith and practice but gives particular attention to that of consumerism. He writes, "This is a far more heinous and insidious challenge to the gospel, because in so many ways it infects each and every one of us."

59. Pastoring, the life and work of the clergy, was often described and conceived of as sharing in the shepherding care and ministry of Christ. Christ being the chief shepherd. See Allen, *The Ministry of the Church*. For a contemporary reflection on the nature of pastoring, see Dawn and Peterson, *The Unnecessary Pastor*.

60. Spiritual direction, especially in contemporary understandings, focuses on the work of the director in listening to both the directee, the individual seeking guidance, and to God. See Guenther, *Holy Listening*. Spiritual direction often involves issues of discernment. Discernment is a prayerful consideration of a decision. The desire is to seek God's will for the decision. See Liebert, *The Art of Discernment*.

Christian educators (catechesis[61] and discipleship)[62] have not always served the Church well. In their own way, all these practitioners share in each other's work from the perspective of developing the spiritual lives of the people they serve.

Lay and ordained ministers teach others the basics of their faith. They catechize. They also guide others in following Jesus Christ. Spiritual directors also engage in the work of catechesis and discipleship. Christian lay ministers and educators exercise their own forms of pastoral leadership and care in their work. The great mystics and teachers of Christian history were all engaged in the foundational work of spiritual formation. Spiritual formation in an increasingly secular age should be a shared foundational emphasis of all Christian scholars, ministers, spiritual directors, and educators. The method of practical spiritual theology encourages partnerships between scholars and practitioners of these fields. Such partnerships will facilitate the ends of practical spiritual theology by resourcing and inspiring the spiritual lives of Christians in the present through the writings of the Christian mystics of the past.

PRACTICAL SPIRITUAL THEOLOGY

It may be helpful to understand spiritual theology using practical theological terms.[63] For example, spiritual theology draws upon the experience of

---

61. Basic instruction in the faith. Historically, in preparing individuals for baptism. For historical and liturgical considerations see Chupungco, *Handbook for Liturgical Studies*, 14. For a contemporary approach to retrieving the ancient model of catechesis in Christian communities, see Bushofsky et al., *Go Make Disciples: An Invitation to Baptismal Living*.

62. The following of Jesus, being a student of Jesus in all aspects of one's life. Discipleship is sometimes conceived of as life in Christ. See Gatta, *Life in Christ*. Discipleship has its roots in Scripture when Jesus' invited the first apostles to, "Come follow me" (Matt 4:19) and in the words of the Great Commission given by Jesus, "Now the eleven disciples went to Galilee, to the mountain to which Jesus had directed them. When they saw him, they worshiped him; but some doubted. And Jesus came and said to them, "All authority in heaven and on earth has been given to me. Go therefore and make disciples of all nations, baptizing them in the name of the Father and of the Son and of the Holy Spirit, and teaching them to obey everything that I have commanded you. And remember, I am with you always, to the end of the age" (Matt 28:16–20).

63. This possibility presents itself in the definition of spiritual theology given earlier by Simon Chan, specifically, "Spiritual theology seeks to understand spiritual growth from beginning to end, making use of biblical and *experiential* data." Chan, *Spiritual Theology*, 18. Emphasis mine.

Christians seeking union with God. In this light, one might conceive of spiritual theology as a type of normative and confessional practical theology. Many traditional approaches to theology are normative. In these approaches, theology is utilized to develop norms, standards, and boundaries for belief and practice. For example, a theology of marriage or a theology of preaching. Theology is often done through a particular confessional or perspective of faith, such as Anglican theology or Roman Catholic theology. Whereas much of practical theology is more descriptive than prescriptive, while also more suggestive than normative.[64] Such theology tends to describe the beliefs and practices of a given Christian community versus prescribing beliefs and practices for a specific Christian community. Spiritual theology tends to be a prescriptive discipline that presents norms for the spiritual life. Like practical theology, it is also possible to think of local spiritual theologies as offering conclusions directed at a specific context and only tentatively suggested for wider audiences. For example, a practical theology of spiritual direction for African American communities.[65]

To disregard spiritual theology is to dismiss the wisdom, practice, and religious experience of Christians across the centuries. To disregard spiritual theology may be to disregard God. If mystics like Hilton and others have encountered God or helped others to encounter God, to disregard spiritual theology is at the least to disregard the testimony of those who have encountered God. For these reasons and others, Christian scholars and practitioners should become familiar with spiritual theology. To include ascetical and mystical expressions of spiritual theology. This will broaden and deepen the counsel they give to those they teach and serve. The goal of practical spiritual theology is to do spiritual theology by bringing the writings of a mystic in conversation with the experiences of contemporary believers. In this way, the emphasis on studying human experience and practice in partnership with the social sciences from practical theology joins together with the wisdom and guidance found in spiritual theology.

For much of Western Christian history up to the time of Hilton, the pursuit of faith was often understood as having two pathways: the active life and the contemplative life. The story of Mary and Martha has been interpreted over the centuries as illustrating these two pathways. Martha represents the active life and Mary the contemplative. Generally, interpreters

---

64. Cahalan and Mikoski, *Opening the Field of Practical*, 4.
65. Peacock, *Soul Care in African American Practice*.

judged Jesus' words "Mary has chosen the better part"[66] as affirming the superiority of the contemplative life.[67] The contemplative is more attuned to the interior life of prayer and union with God.[68] It is a focus on the believer's inner experience with God, both cognitively and affectively. The experience of God in heart and mind. The active being more attuned to obligations to love God by caring for or being in right relationship with one's neighbors. The interior life, being the focus of the contemplative life, is critically relevant to a theology of action—a prime concern of practical theology.[69] How is the Christian life to be lived? Is action the central and fundamental way of understanding what it means to be a Christian? Is a Christian one who acts by loving God and loving others? Or is a Christian one who abides with God and in others in love? Is love the central and fundamental way of understanding what it means to be a Christian?

A focus on the contemplative life and being is an important corrective to church and society's focus on ceaseless activity and doing. The two pathways, active and contemplative, are both necessary, sometimes for individuals, but always for the entire Christian community. Both pathways, in their medieval conceptions, stress relationship with God as the primary relationship that makes all actions and all other relationships ultimately meaningful. Without God as the central goal of the spiritual life, its associated practices become means to various good ends such as better living, social justice, and flourishing congregations. However, this is an inversion of a central claim of the Christian mystical tradition as embodied by Hilton, namely that the pursuit of God for God's sake is the goal of the Christian faith.[70] This pursuit may involve improved living, flourishing congregations, and the pursuit of social justice. However, one pursues these outcomes as

---

66. Luke 10:42.

67. See Thomas Aquinas' discussion of this matter affirming the traditional position of the superiority of the contemplative life: *Summa Theologiae* 2.2.179–81. For a contrary view, see Meister Eckhart's discussion of Luke 10:38–42. Walshe, *The Complete Mystical Works of Meister Eckhart*, 83–90.

68. Jeffery, *Toward a Perfect Love*, xxi.

69. Heitink, *Practical Theology*, 101–3.

70. Allen writes, "What is the goal of the spiritual life? This goal has been described in various ways—as the vision of God, the vision of the Trinity, union with God, participation in God's life and being, the pure love of God, and the condition of knowing and enjoying God forever." Allen. *Spiritual Theology*, 23. Chan writes, "The Christian life is an intentional process aimed at a goal that is various called union with God (Catholic), deification (Orthodox) and glorification (Protestant)." Chan, *Spiritual Theology*, 18.

part of the pursuit of God or in response to an encounter with God. Thus, God becomes the end and not only a means of the spiritual life.

WALTER HILTON

One way of doing practical spiritual theology would be to do an extensive study of the mystics across the centuries. Such a study would include creating a synthesis of their principles and direction for the spiritual life and bringing this synthesis into conversation with the experience of contemporary believers. This could be a fruitful approach and the voluminous works of a scholar like Bernard McGinn make such a project feasible.[71] This was also the approach taken by many mystical writers through the centuries. However, practical spiritual theology offers a means of retrieving and reviving the writings and teachings of specific mystics for the benefit of those seeking to live the spiritual life today. The advantage of this approach over a larger synthesis is that it takes each voice seriously in its own right. It allows contemporary Christians to encounter another human being as a fellow witness to the faith, rather than simply following a set of abstracted principles. Also, practical theology is oriented toward the particular, helping one to focus on specific contexts versus creating theological systems that attempt to universalize. When theological principles are generalized across several contexts, differences may be glossed over. Often differences are related to particular contexts and situations. Giving attention to specifics of a situation, theology, or community can enrich theological reflection, instead of flattening it through generalization.[72]

Walter Hilton is an ideal subject for the development of practical spiritual theology because his teachings reflect a systematic concern for the spiritual life while being directed toward specific individuals and settings. Hilton's work has been described as a "summa of the spiritual life" because of its comprehensive character and because his teaching builds upon the spiritual theology from the past centuries up to his own time.[73] In this way, one could describe Hilton as a nascent practical spiritual theologian in so far as he brings the historical witness and insight of spiritual theology into

---

71. See McGinn's series, The Presence of God: A History of Western Christian Mysticism. Of particular interest for this work is McGinn, *The Varieties of Vernacular Mysticism: 1350–1550*, 331–470.

72. Nancy Moules et al., *Conducting Hermeneutic Research*, 63–65.

73. Thornton, *English Spirituality*, 176–77.

conversation with the experience of Christians of his own time. Hilton did not engage in formal qualitative study in his ministry of writing and spiritual direction. Such methods were unavailable to him and other historic mystics. However, Hilton, like spiritual directors before him and following, did engage in qualitative study in an informal sense. He reflected on his own experience and the experience of those he worked with to gain insight and offer better counsel. The method of practical spiritual theology can be used to enrich the practice of ministry, spiritual direction, and education in a variety of ways, by practitioners and communities. A method that gives attention to a particular mystic, their teachings, and how the mystic's writings relate to contemporary ideas, situations, and people. Before giving attention to one mystic, Walter Hilton, further consideration will be given to the authority of mystics within the Christian tradition.

AUTHORITATIVE EXPERIENCE: WHY LISTEN TO MYSTICS?

In the history of the Church, the experience and practice of mystics, spiritual teachers and saints has been authoritative. An authority given to mystics by virtue of their experience with the holy.[74] Their experience with the presence of God. This authority was often complementary to the teaching authority of the Church. At times mystical authority was a challenge to the teaching authority of the Church. For example, Catherine of Siena, the fourteenth-century Italian mystic, was able to critique Church leaders and practice in ways that most women, and many men, could not, because of her reputation for holiness, among other factors.[75] Mystics sometimes experience tension between the Church's authority and their own experiences with God. Julian of Norwich wrestles in her writings regarding the relationship between the revelations she received from God about love and the teachings of the Church about eternal punishment.[76] The conflicted and often inhumane history of how the Church responded to medieval women mystics illustrates the tensions between Church's institutional authority and the mystics' experiential authority.[77]

74. Otto, *The Idea of the Holy*.
75. F. Thomas Luongo, *The Saint Politics of Catherine of Siena*.
76. Rolf, *Julian's Gospel*, 407.
77. Margery Kempe, a near contemporary of Walter Hilton, experienced intense scrutiny about her spiritual activities. The book about her life, written by her or dictated

This experiential authority of mystics was tied to how others perceived them. Specifically, in how those around the mystic perceived them as being examples of holiness or sanctity. As conceived by Hilton, holiness in the spiritual life is a life of virtue and prayerful union with God. Holiness is often associated with mystics, as well as other exemplary Christians, sometimes called saints. While there is the Biblical understanding of all believers being saints in Jesus Christ.[78] The New Testament also holds up certain individuals as being exceptional followers of Jesus.[79] Over time, for many, the term saint came to be associated with exceptional individuals, instead of Christians in general. The concept of holiness is Scriptural, first appearing in the Old Testament. In the Old Testament holiness expresses the state of being set apart.[80]

The people of Israel were set apart from their neighbors by the observance of certain rituals and moral commandments. Israel's set apart status, being different from their neighbor nations, was understood as reflecting the holiness of God. "You are to be holy to me because I, the LORD, am holy, and I have set you apart from the nations to be my own."[81] This was a communal holiness, by which the people of God reflected the holiness of God. Holiness was the focus of the community over that of the individual. This book assumes the reality of God. However, it is necessary for the concept of holiness and related mystical experiences to be investigated from other perspectives.[82] Theological approaches to mysticism and spirituality can benefit from the work of other methods of inquiry. For example, reading the work of a historian who describes the major events of the period of history in which a mystic lived helps the theologian to situate the mystic's teachings within a given time and place.

---

by her, contains recollections of many encounters with Church authorities. See Kempe, *The Book of Margery Kempe*. The Church's heinous failures in the treatment of women reporting or asserting spiritual experiences are well known. Women being interrogated about their visions and spiritual experiences risked being identified not as mystics of God but as messengers of Satan with disastrous results. See Elliot, *Proving Woman*.

78. Acts 9:32, 1 Cor 1:2.

79. Heb 11.

80. Hill and Walton, *A Survey of the Old Testament*, 132–33.

81. Lev 20:26.

82. This approach was taken by William James who concluded after his seminal study, "I feel bound to say that religious experience, as we have studied it, cannot be cited as unequivocally supporting the infinitist belief. The only thing that it unequivocally testifies to is that we can experience union with something larger than ourselves and in that union find our greatest peace." James, *The Varieties of Religious Experience*, 468.

Foundations of Practical Spiritual Theology

MYSTICS AND SAINTS: IMITATORS OF CHRIST

Saints are exemplars, extraordinary examples, of the Christian faith. They are noted for their holiness of life. A life of prayer and virtue. Some writers use the term sanctification instead of holiness. Either term may describe the pursuit of and state of being Christ-like. This holiness takes place within a community but includes concern for individual virtue. It is a process made possible by and driven by grace.[83] The fruits of the Spirit in the New Testament are markers of individual holiness, "But the fruits of the spirit are love, joy, peace, forbearance, kindness, goodness, faithfulness, gentleness and self-control."[84] Today, holiness often carries—from its Biblical roots—the idea of living a rigorously moral life. A life set apart. Sometimes, holiness is associated with a sense of the numinous being present in an individual. Such that encountering this individual is akin to encountering the numinous.[85] In Christian understanding, this experience is preeminent in encountering Christ. Jesus said, "Anyone who has seen me, has seen the Father."[86] Jesus is God in the flesh. To encounter Christ is to encounter God. Peter, one of the original twelve apostles, after meeting Jesus for the first time demonstrates an awareness of the moral excellence of Christ when he says, "Lord, go away from me; I am a sinful man."[87] These two elements of holiness—moral and numinous—come together in the understanding of what it means to be a saint. The saint reflects the moral excellence and numinous reality of Jesus. However much a saint reflects the reality of Jesus they are still human. They have flaws. They are people of their time. Contemporary Christians seeking to learn from the mystics and saints will need tools of affirmation and tools of critique. This reflects a synthesis of the affirmative and critical approaches of both practical theology and spiritual theology.

The history of Christian spirituality acknowledges that saints may come from a wide variety of life situations, not just the monastery.[88] For centuries, spiritual teachers and directors overly emphasized monastic

---

83. Chan, *Spiritual Theology*, 83–84.

84. Gal 5:22–23.

85. This idea might further develop by conceptualizing holy persons as holy places. Such that encountering a saint is akin to visiting a holy place.

86. John 14:9.

87. Luke 5:8.

88. For examples, see Foster, *Streams of Living Water*, 303–78.

holiness, excluding other Christians to a secondary spiritual status. While this was true of many times and places, it has also been true that monastic and non-monastic forms of spirituality have existed alongside and interacted with each other for centuries.[89] Not only have saints—married, single, or monastic—embodied a certain moral excellence and closeness to the divine[90] but they have also brought the experience of God to others in unique ways. Archbishop and theologian Michael Ramsey defines a saint as "one who has a strange nearness to God and makes God real and near to other people."[91] The saint is not only morally excellent and close to God—her or his presence communicates the reality of the divine to other human beings. Human beings who may be far from being saints or mystics themselves.[92]

How does a human become a mystic or saint? On one hand, the human being can only receive what God gives. Mystical experience or saintliness is a grace, a free gift given by God to a human being. On the other hand, human beings can open themselves to God in ways that facilitate the gifting of mystical experience and saintly virtue. This is the process of Christian growth, the pursuit of holiness or sanctification, which human beings can pursue in cooperation with the power and presence of the Holy Spirit. "Sanctification is the process" by which human beings actually begin to become holy, free of the effects of evil and full of charity or divine love."[93] This process is God driven, as attested to by many of the great saints, including Walter Hilton. Human beings can prepare themselves for an experience of God and growth in God through certain practices, including certain ritual practices. "Ascetical theology is concerned with disciplines and practices that will allow God's grace to become more effective" in human lives.[94] Certain practices and rituals can be means of facilitating the work of the

89. Peters, *The Story of Monasticism*, 187.

90. The concept of the divine or numinous is analogous in some respects to Paul Tillich's conception, "The dimension of ultimate reality is the dimension of the Holy." Tillich, *The Essential*, 49.

91. Dales, *Glory Descending*, 149.

92. This lends further worth to an investigation of holy persons as holy places. If a saint is a person who helps to make the numinous real for others, then a certain power or heightened presence of the numinous attached or embodied in the saint that is able to capture the attention of individuals who normally are not aware of God. In other words, there is something "more," something "overtly spiritual" that communicates to less actively spiritual individuals when they visit a holy place or meet a holy person. What is that something more?

93. Allen, *Spiritual Theology*, 9.

94. Allen, *Spiritual Theology*, 67.

Holy Spirit. All saints and Christian mystics engage in religious practice and rituals of some kind. This is obvious. What is more complicated is the relationship between spiritual practice and holiness. Do religious practices, including ritual practices, contribute to the development of holiness? Most human beings, including most Christians, engage in religious practice, including rituals, yet few are recognized as saints or persons of extraordinary merit.

Is it that saints engage in certain rituals and practices that most people are unaware of? Such that saints form a sort of secret society, passing down the secret rituals and practices, of which they alone have access? Is it the frequency of their participation in religious practices? The mystic or saint is a person who may live a highly ritualized or to say it differently, highly practiced life. This does not necessarily mean a life of highly formalized religious ritual or practice. The saint lives a life of interior and exterior disposition toward God. Religious practices enable human beings to enter different mindsets, facilitating different behaviors and attitudes about the world. Rituals are psycho-social exercises that can train human beings into diverse ways of being and doing in the world. In this way, religious practice may be conceived of more broadly than specifically religious rituals.

Transformative practice may manifest in ritual-like activities, including formal prayer, but also ways of responding to people and situations that directly reflect Christian commitments to love, serve, and forgive. For example, through the practice of intentional, conscious interaction, and desiring in those interactions to demonstrate the love of God, a corporate executive may pursue holiness in the context of her corporate office. For her, the ritual action may be in a quiet moment at her desk or in cultivating an awareness of the holy in each person she meets. In this way, her corporate office becomes a context for pursuing a life of holiness, just as a monk may pursue holiness in the context of his monastery. Theologian Nathan Mitchell writes that "ritual was not primarily a symbol system aimed at the production of meaning but a technology . . . aimed at the production of a virtuous self . . . of a person who is obedient, humble, chaste, charitable, compassionate, hospitable, and wise."[95] The idea of ritual and practice, especially in a monastic setting, being a technology for self-development is

---

95. Bradshaw and Melloh, *Foundations in Ritual Studies*, 105. In fact, the Church has a vast treasure trove of these technologies, which have been the study of ascetical and mystical theology, often referred to today as spiritual theology.

ancient.[96] The saint as gifted and guided by God utilizes the practices of the spiritual life as a "technology of the self," leading to personal transformation and a Christ-likeness. Hilton and other mystics are teachers of these "technologies of the self." Ascetical theology is the historic Christian discipline of pursuing transformation in cooperation with God by using a variety of technologies of the self, such as prayer, fasting, and almsgiving. Ascetical theology, one part of spiritual theology, focuses on the practices, rituals, spiritual exercises that can help the Christian grow, through God's grace, into greater measures of Christlikeness. These transformative practices can facilitate an individual's openness toward union with God.

Saints continue to be recognized by acclamation. That is, other Christians notice their unusual virtues and connection with God and begin to honor them. Often a saint is first honored locally before their reputation spreads. Most liturgical denominations have official processes for saints to be recognized. Once recognized the saint is given a date on the denomination's calendar for remembrance and celebration. For example, Walter Hilton is honored annually on March 24 on the Church of England's liturgical calendar.[97] The Roman Catholic Church has one of the most formal and prolonged processes for this recognition. A process called canonization. Popular acclamation of a saint usually precedes the formal recognition process of a denomination. Sometimes a saint is honored locally and never formally. In both processes, Christians at large, as well as denominational committees, have usually used the criteria of moral excellence and the experience of God in recognizing and celebrating saints.[98]

Based on their own experiences with God, saints and mystics have been recognized as authorities. Authorities on the reality of God and the paths to God. For these and other reasons, mystics, saints, and spiritual teachers warrant contemporary attention. From a practical spiritual theological perspective, they warrant attention because they can resource and inspire contemporary faith and practice. The world is still a sometimes cold and dark place. The need for spiritual bonfires—lives that witness to the warm presence of God—remains high. The history of the Christian faith demonstrates that one small fire of faith can kindle another fire of faith.

---

96. Bradshaw and Melloh, *Foundations in Ritual Studies*, 110.

97. Simon Kershaw, *Exciting Holiness*, 140.

98. Episcopal Church *Lesser Feasts and Fasts*, V. "What we celebrate in the lives of the saints is the presence of Christ expressing itself in and through particular lives lived in the midst of specific historical circumstances."

Empowered by the Holy Spirit, Christians pass on the fire of their faith to others until a family, community, or even the world shines with the love of God. This growth in holiness is a participation in the saving and glorifying work of Jesus Christ, who said, "I am the light of the world."[99] God is the great fire.[100] The hearts of humanity are altars that can remain cold and bare or they can become altars lit with flames warm and bright. The mystics are the great firekeepers.

---

99. Heb 12:29. "For indeed our God is a consuming fire."

Chapter 2

WALTER HILTON
A Resource for Practical Spiritual Theology

HILTON'S LIFE AND WORKS

Walter Hilton was an Augustinian canon,[1] spiritual director, and writer in fourteenth-century England. It was a time of social and ecclesial upheaval. The Black Death, which raged throughout the century, killed upwards of half the population.[2] John Wycliffe's Lollard movement, a precursor to the Protestant Reformation, was a constant source of controversy.[3] Hilton's own prior at Thurgarton was authorized to arrest Lollards.[4] The Peasant Revolt of 1381, prompted by high taxes and dissatisfaction with the serfdom system, was marked by bloodshed.[5] The One Hundred Years War with France was in progress, which contributed to the high taxation.[6] It was also a time of mystics and monastics. Hilton, and near contemporaries

---

1. Jeffery, *Toward a Perfect Love*, xix. Canons were semi-monastic, lived in community, and often served the pastoral needs of the local community. Jeffery writes, "Canons were involved in the ordinary day-to-day workings of the community. Hilton would have had every reason to be familiar with the market life of his village, labor in the fields, and the ordinary necessities of rural and small-town life." The canons were different, though related, to the Austin Friars, sharing a common heritage in St. Augustine. See Laferriere, "The Austin Friars in Pre-Reformation England."
2. Hatcher, *The Black Death*, xi.
3. Clark and Dorward, *Walter Hilton: The Scale of Perfection*, 30.
4. Kerchberger, *Walter Hilton: The Goad of Love*, 22–23.
5. Mortimer, *The Time Traveler's Guide to Medieval England*, 51.
6. Allmand, *The Hundred Years War*, 24.

such as Richard Rolle,[7] the unknown author of the *Cloud of Unknowing*,[8] and Julian of Norwich[9] contributed to what is often referred to as the "Golden Age of English Mysticism."[10]

Walter Hilton was born around the year 1340. While not conclusive, it is possible that he was born in the village of Hilton, in Huntingdonshire, England.[11] We know nothing of his parents or family life, though he would have grown up during one of the worst outbreaks of the bubonic plague, the "Black Death." He entered Cambridge around the year 1357. He studied civil and canon law.[12] Civil law was a precursor to the study of canon law in the fourteenth century.[13] It appears that he practiced canon law in the consistory court system for several years.[14] Around 1382, Hilton left the practice of law and became a hermit.[15] Hermits were solitaries. They were not members of religious orders. Hermits committed themselves to lives of prayer and contemplation. Unlike anchorites or anchoresses, such as Julian of Norwich, who remained in one location; hermits, such as Richard Rolle, traveled from place to place. Hilton wrote to his friend and fellow lawyer, Adam Horsley, who was also discerning a religious vocation, "They believe that if you despise the world and dismiss both the study and practice of the law from your mind, cast off honours, degrees and benefices, and choose poverty and humility for Christ's sake, that you are infatuated and insane."[16] In 1386, Hilton entered the community of Augustinian Canons in Thurgarton. He died on the Eve of the Annunciation, March 24, 1396.[17]

All of Hilton's extant writings appear to be dated from the last twenty years of his life. This time span encompasses the final years of his practice of canon law, his time as a hermit, and his life as a canon at the priory in Thurgarton. He wrote most of his works as a hermit and canon. Hilton's

---

7. Allen, *Richard Rolle*.
8. Walsh, *The Cloud of Unknowing*.
9. Julian of Norwich, *Julian of Norwich: Showings*.
10. McGinn, *The Varieties of Vernacular Mysticism*, x.
11. Horobin and Mooney, *Middle English Texts in Translation*, 160.
12. Clark and Dorward, *Walter Hilton: The Scale of Perfection*, 13–14.
13. For an overview of the development and practice of medieval canon law see Rennie, *Medieval Canon Law*.
14. Horobin and Mooney, *Middle English Texts in Translation*, 162.
15. Eric College, *The Mediaeval Mystics of England*, 63.
16. Horobin and Mooney, *Middle English Texts in Translation*, 161.
17. Horobin and Mooney, *Middle English Texts in Translation*, 160.

most well-known and influential work is *The Scale of Perfection*.[18] The work is sometimes also titled, *The Ladder of Perfection*.[19] Hilton wrote the *Scale* to an anchoress. It provides comprehensive instruction on the practices associated with pursuing union with God. His treatise, *The Mixed Life*,[20] is probably the second most well-known and influential of his works. It is written to a layperson with worldly responsibilities seeking direction in living the faith. Hilton wrote a number of other minor works, including *On the Image of Sin* (*De imagine peccati*), *On the Usefulness and Prerogatives of Religion* (*De utilitae et prerogativis religionis*), *Letter to Someone Wanting to Renounce the World* (*Epistola ad quemdam seculo renunciare volentem*), *Conclusions Concerning Images* (*Conclusions de Imaginibus*), and a commentary on Psalm 90. He is sometimes credited with translating *The Goad of Love* (*Stimulus Amoris*) from Latin into Middle English. Scholars disagree as to whether he wrote *On Angels Song* and a commentary on Psalm 91.[21] His works were widely read by religious (vowed members of orders), clergy, and laity. Theologian and priest Julian Gatta tells us, "In the late fourteenth and fifteenth centuries, there was in England no more highly esteemed devotional writer than Walter Hilton."[22]

The popularity of his writings is partially understood by their accessibility. While Hilton wrote some of his minor works in Latin, he wrote *The Scale* and *The Mixed Life* in Middle English. In the fourteenth century, there was a movement toward the use of the vernacular language, coupled with a growing literacy among the educated classes.[23] However, this alone does

---

18. Clark and Dorward, *Walter Hilton: The Scale of Perfection*.

19. In Latin, the word "scale" can be translated as ladder or stairwell. This suggests a familiar monastic image in medieval literature, which is a derivative of Jacob's ladder in Gen 28:10–17, implying stages to heaven or contemplation. *The Ladder of Perfection* rather than *The Scale of Perfection* is sometimes used to refer to this work. However, many scholars, including those who have worked with the Middle English manuscripts—*The Scale* was originally written in Middle English—use the title, *The Scale of Perfection*. See for example Bestul, *Walter Hilton: The Scale of Perfection: Teams*, also Horobin and Mooney, *Middle English Texts in Translation*. Nonetheless, the imagery of a ladder, implying stages of progression toward divine love is an appropriate characterization of the work. "To Hilton, the Christian life is a continuity; there are stages, steps up the ladder of perfection." Thornton, *English Spirituality*, 179.

20. Jeffery, *Toward a Perfect Love*.

21. Clark and Dorward, *Walter Hilton: The Scale of Perfection*, 13–17.

22. Gatta, *Three Spiritual Directors for Our Time*, 17.

23. Fanous and Gillespie, *The Cambridge Companion to Medieval English Mysticism*, xii.

not account for his influence. The impact of his work must also be attributed to his insightful, pastoral, and comprehensive approach. Theologian and religious historian Bernard McGinn writes, "Walter Hilton is usually judged to provide a balanced and accessible introduction to the mystical life."[24] Theologian and priest Martin Thorton tells us, "Walter Hilton, Austin Canon Regular of Thurgarton, near Southwell, is at the centre of English ascetical theology, and remains, to my mind, our prime source of teaching on spiritual direction."[25] Literature scholar David L. Jeffery, commenting on his insight, writes, "Hilton is one of the great psychologists of the Christian spiritual tradition. He is pragmatic, a spiritual realist."[26] Lastly, medieval literature scholar Joy Russell-Smith attributes much of Hilton's influence to his willingness to encourage serious prayer and spirituality among the laity, "Hilton was exceptional among writers of his time in giving close attention to the problems of the contemplative life in an active state."[27] Hilton's influence, style, and breadth make him an ideal candidate for the development of practical spiritual theology.

THEOLOGICAL VISION

Hilton's vision of the spiritual life is shaped and situated within the Augustinian tradition.[28] Augustine of Hippo's historic influence on Western Christianity is pervasive.[29] While Thomas Aquinas was emerging as an authority during Hilton's lifetime,[30] Augustine remained fixed as the authority in the theological tradition. Hilton had committed himself to the Augustinian way, by joining a community of canons specifically committed to *The Rule of St. Augustine*.[31] In England, the tradition of spiritual direction was influenced not only by St. Augustine, but by other great spiritual writers,

---

24. McGinn, *The Varieties of Vernacular Mysticism*, 340.
25. Thornton, *English Spirituality*, 176.
26. Jeffery, *Toward a Perfect Love*, xxiv.
27. Walsh, *Pre-Reformation English Spirituality*, 196.
28. Raitt, *Christian Spirituality*, 196.
29. Clark and Dorward, *Walter Hilton: The Scale of Perfection*, 22.
30. Clark and Dorward, *Walter Hilton: The Scale of Perfection*, 24.
31. Van Bavel, *The Rule of St. Augustine*. A rule of life is a routine of spiritual observance and practice, often associated with communities of vowed religious. There are several monastic rules of life. One of the most influential monastic rules of life, written in the sixth century, is *The Rule of St. Benedict*. See Fry et al., *The Rule of St. Benedict*.

who like Hilton, were Augustinian canons, such as Richard and Hugh of St. Victor.[32] Hilton was part of the cenobitic way. The life of vowed members of religious communities. Hilton was also an inheritor and participant in a distinctively English eremitical tradition. The eremitical way was the solitary path to God. The life of anchoresses like Julian of Norwich and hermits like Richard Rolle are notable examples. Some of the influencers and proponents of these traditions were Anslem of Canterbury, Aeldred of Rievaulx, and the unknown author of *Ancrene Wisse*.[33] A monastic rule of guidance for anchoresses. Hilton also engages directly with the ideas of his near contemporary, the hermit and writer, Richard Rolle.[34] This English tradition of mysticism and spiritual direction drew upon earlier eremitical and cenobitic[35] traditions, including Augustine, but developed over time to constitute its own school of thought and practice.[36]

Scholars and translators of fourteenth-century mystical texts John Clark and Rosemary Dorward identify Augustine's *On the Trinity* as being particularly influential on Hilton, "in which the doctrine of the Trinity is integrated with the whole theological perspective of creation and redemption. Throughout his writings, Hilton recalls points found in this book."[37] The spiritual life for Hilton is a participation in and pursuit of union with the Triune God. The human potential for union with God is inherent in the image of God in each human being, the *imago dei*.[38] This image has been tarnished by sin and is in need of restoration. The *imago dei* can be contrasted with the *imago peccati*, the image of sin. Hilton writes, "This is the image that I have spoken of. The image of God in the first creation—was wonderfully bright and fair, full of burning love and spiritual light, but

---

32. Thornton, *English Spirituality*, 110, 117.

33. Julia Lamm, *Christian Mysticism*, 358.

34. Clark and Dorward, *Walter Hilton: The Scale of Perfection*, 24.

35. Eremitical monasticism is solitary; whereas; cenobitic is communal. Eremetical monasticism was common in the Christian East, but also during this period in England. While beyond the scope of this work, tracing connections between eremitical monasticism in the east with eremitical practice in England might be a fruitful and insightful study. Also, eremitical monasticism was an important feature of the Irish Church in earlier centuries. This influenced the development of eremitical monasticism in England. "These Irish monks and anchorites would exert a powerful influence on Anglo-Saxon England." Riehle, *The Secret Within*, 5.

36. Lamm, *Christian Mysticism*, 358.

37. Clark and Dorward, *Walter Hilton: The Scale of Perfection*, 24.

38. "So God created humankind in his image, in the image of God he created them; male and female he created them" (Gen 1:27).

through the sin of the first man, Adam, it was deformed and changed into another likeness."[39] This image can only be restored through Christ, "Since our Lord Jesus . . . died thus for the salvation of man's soul, it was just that sin should be forgiven, and that man's soul (which was his image) should become capable of reformation and restoration to the first likeness, and to the bliss of heaven." [40]

A key concept in Hilton's theology of the spiritual life is that the reforming of the image of God comes in two kinds, "The first, which is reforming in faith alone, is sufficient for salvation; the second is worthy of surpassing reward in the bliss of heaven."[41] Hilton links reforming in faith with the beginner and proficient stages of the spiritual life and reforming in feeling with the third, that of the perfect.[42] The beginner in the spiritual life is pursuing purgation, the stage of the spiritual life dedicated to overcoming sin and building virtue. The proficient in the spiritual life has by God's grace and prayerful effort reached the stage of illumination, the stage of deeper prayer and spiritual experience. No one reaches the fullness of the perfect stage in this life. However, those in this stage are beginning to enter a unitive relationship with God.[43] Hilton's spiritual direction assumes the traditional distinctions between the active and contemplative life.[44] Actives are those who ordinarily are reformed in faith alone. The spiritual life for actives is focused on the love of neighbor, through the traditional works of corporal and spiritual mercy.[45] Contemplatives are those who actively

---

39. Clark and Dorward, *Walter Hilton: The Scale of Perfection*, 193.

40. Clark and Dorward, *Walter Hilton: The Scale of Perfection*, 200.

41. Clark and Dorward, *Walter Hilton: The Scale of Perfection*, 199.

42. Clark and Dorward, *Walter Hilton: The Scale of Perfection*, 200. These stages are employed extensively in spiritual theology and in the writings of various ancient and medieval mystics.

43. Thornton, *English Spirituality*, 12, 17, 22. "A good deal of ascetical-theology . . . comes down to us in the form of 'progressions' . . . The Three Ways of Purgation, Illumination and Union are fundamental to Catholic spirituality; St Thomas makes them personal with the classification Beginners, Proficients and Perfect." See Aquinas, *Summa Theologica*, II–II.183.4.

44. Jeffery, *Toward a Perfect Love*, xx–xxi.

45. Clark and James, *Pastoral Care in Medieval England*. The Works of Corporeal Mercy: 1) To Feed the Hungry, 2) To give drink to the thirsty, 3) To clothe the naked, 4) To Harbor the harborless/Shelter the Homeless, 5) To visit the sick, 6) To ransom the captive/Visit the Imprisoned, 7) To bury the dead. The Spiritual Works of Mercy 1) To instruct the ignorant, 2) To counsel the doubtful, 3) To admonish sinners, 4) To bear wrongs patiently, 5) To forgive offenses willingly, 6) To comfort the afflicted, 7) To pray

seek, through a life of prayer and renunciation, mystical union with God. Reforming in faith and reforming in feeling both require grace-filled ascetical practice. The word ascetical comes from the Greek term *askesis*, meaning exercise. Hence, ascetical theology's concern with spiritual exercise and practice. These exercises and practices are rooted in God's grace and facilitate growth and progression in the spiritual life. The need for exercise or spiritual discipline is also attested to in Scripture,

> Do you not know that in a race all the runners run, but only one gets the prize? Run in such a way as to get the prize. Everyone who competes in the games goes into strict training. They do it to get a crown that will not last, but we do it to get a crown that will last forever. Therefore I do not run like someone running aimlessly; I do not fight like a boxer beating the air. No, I strike a blow to my body and make it my slave so that after I have preached to others, I myself will not be disqualified for the prize.[46]

The prize in Hilton's conception of the spiritual life is God and specifically union with God through contemplation.[47] Hilton follows Augustinian theology and anthropology in understanding the human soul as a created trinity, whose three faculties (memory, reason, will) reflect the three persons of the Trinity. The fall has removed from human beings both an intuitive awareness of God and a natural conformity to following God's will. The spiritual life and its end, union with God, seek to restore this awareness and conformity.[48] This gift of contemplation is pursued through the three traditional stages of the mystical life: the purgative, the illuminative, and the unitive.[49] Hilton recognizes that "Reforming in fullness cannot be had in this life, but it is postponed after this life to the glory of heaven."[50]

MAJOR EMPHASES

Hilton is rigorously Christocentric in his theology, centering the pursuit of the spiritual life in the person and work of Jesus Christ. The reformation of the image of God is related to the individual's relationship with the

---

for the living and the dead.
46. 1 Cor 9:24–27 (New International Version).
47. Clark and Dorward, *Walter Hilton: The Scale of Perfection*, 36.
48. Clark and Dorward, *Walter Hilton: The Scale of Perfection*, 36.
49. Thornton, *English Spirituality*, 22.
50. Clark and Dorward, *Walter Hilton: The Scale of Perfection*, 198.

Lord, "For as long as he does not find his image reformed in you he is a stranger to you, and far away."[51] The spiritual life's goal of union with God is not merely a state of purity or perfection for Hilton, but is a personal experience of Jesus Christ, drawing closer and closer to the individual. The reformation of the soul is ultimately a pursuit of Christ-likeness, "There is no virtue you can practice . . . able to make you resemble our Lord without humility and charity."[52] This emphasis on Christ was not always present in the writings of Hilton's day. For example, Hilton makes several editorial adjustments, as well as additions, in his translation of *The Goad of Love*, but one of the most telling is his "addition of many Christocentric passages. This procedure has been found to have been carried out deliberately and in great detail throughout his translation." [53]

Hilton is open to and encouraging of lay spirituality. His writings were popular with the laity, religious, and clergy. In traditional ascetical or spiritual theology, a serious spiritual life was thought only possible by retreating from the world in the eremitical or cenobitic fashion. In *The Scale of Perfection*, book one, Hilton reaffirms this notion. However, in book two, written sometime later, Hilton seems open to the possibility of the laity pursuing the contemplative life in some measure. Further, Hilton's actual guidance to laypeople, as found in *The Mixed Life* and *Someone Wanting to Renounce the World*, not only consider the possibility of serious lay spirituality, but by implication may suggest a critique of the contemplative life as the normative standard for mature faith and practice.[54] For Hilton, an individual's state in life is determinative of how they should live their faith. Hilton commends a third option, between that of the active and contemplative lives, what he calls the mixed life.

Earlier writers like Gregory the Great and Augustine commended this path for bishops and pastors, but Hilton innovates by suggesting that the mixed life is appropriate for "both those who would be pastors and those who are disposed to positions of secular responsibility."[55] In writing to a

---

51. Clark and Dorward, *Walter Hilton: The Scale of Perfection*, 123.
52. Clark and Dorward, *Walter Hilton: The Scale of Perfection*, 123.
53. Kerchberger, *Walter Hilton: The Goad of Love*, 51.
54. Hilton's praise for the mixed life and opening it to laypeople with worldly responsibilities is an indirect critique of the contemplative life. It may be a theological move his readers could make. Even as he continued in various writings, as did other spiritual writers of his age, to maintain the contemplative life as ideal. Interestingly, Hilton himself, as an Austin Canon would have lived the mixed life, not the contemplative life.
55. Jeffery, *Toward a Perfect Love*, 11.

powerful man, who was wondering if he should abandon his business and familial responsibilities in favor of the contemplative life, Hilton writes, "You must not altogether follow your said desire in giving over or neglecting those businesses and cares of the world that are necessary, and do belong to you, either for your upholding . . . or in the ruling of other persons or things that pertain to your charge."[56] Hilton argues that those who abandon their responsibilities or relationships in order to pursue God, "do not fulfill the law of love."[57] Hilton lifts up Jesus as an example of the mixed life,

> At times he communed and mixed with people, showing to them his deeds of mercy. He taught . . . he visited the sick and healed . . . he fed the hungry . . . and he comforted . . . At other times he broke away from . . . all worldly folk, and of his disciples . . . and went alone into the desert . . . and continued there all night in prayer.[58]

Hilton's recognition of the realities of the lives of lay people, filled with relationships and responsibilities, combined with his insistence that a serious spiritual life could be lived "in the world" no doubt contributed to his popularity as a devotional writer. The concept of being in the world but not of the world is derived from Scripture.[59] Taking religious vows and entering a monastery was understood as leaving the world. Lay people by definition remained within the everyday world outside of the monastery.

Hilton is rigorously Biblical in his theology and in his spiritual direction. For those able, he commended the reading of Holy Scripture. The reading of Holy Scripture by the laity and in the vernacular was still controversial in Hilton's time. The Lollard movement, which was condemned as heretical, and which Hilton's own community in Thurgarton was familiar with, was to many an example of the dangers of encouraging both lay spirituality and Bible reading.[60] Hilton avoids these dangers by assuming "an ecclesial and Christological basis for Bible reading."[61] The spiritual life is to be pursued within the life, teachings, and practices of the Church.[62] Hilton's writings are filled with Biblical quotations and allusions. He employs

---

56. Plantinga, *Walter Hilton: Treatise Written to a Devout Man*, 3.
57. Jeffery, *Toward a Perfect Love*, 11.
58. Jeffery, *Toward a Perfect Love*, 11.
59. John 17:14–15.
60. Fanous, *Medieval English Mysticism*, 119–120.
61. Clark and Dorward, *Walter Hilton: The Scale of Perfection*, 38.
62. Clark and Dorward, *Walter Hilton: The Scale of Perfection*, 38.

the traditional medieval understanding of Scripture: the literal, moral, allegorical, and analogical.[63] Meditation, *meditatio*, on Scriptural texts, a classic practice of the contemplative life, is commended by Hilton.[64] Regular engagement with Scripture, for those able to read, was recommended as a powerful means of facilitating personal transformation and an encounter with God.[65]

Hilton warns against the limits of Biblical knowledge in terms of attaining the goals of the spiritual life, "This knowledge is good, and it may be called a part of contemplation . . . Yet this kind of knowledge is common to good and bad, because it may be had without charity."[66] Here again, Hilton stresses the relational nature of the spiritual life. Knowledge, whether Biblical or otherwise, is helpful in so much that it facilitates love toward God and neighbor.[67] Also, the personal knowledge of Christ, received through the reformation of the image of God in an individual, can only be achieved through God's gift in concert with human receptivity.[68] The spiritual theology of Walter Hilton, like most ascetical and mystical theology, is founded on grace and not works. Martin Thornton highlights this point,

> Are not fasts, methods, physical disciplines, offices, and prayers, nothing but a system of justification by works? The answer is 'no', because grace is love and the quest for love is not a justifying work but an ultimate end. We arrive at the conclusion that the ascetic starts with the assumption of prevenient grace, that it assumes not only the good works do not justify but that, without grace, they are impossible. The whole of ascetical theology consists in the quest for, and respond to, grace which is the love of God.[69]

This follows the teachings of the Apostle Paul in the New Testament, "For by grace you have been saved through faith, and this is not your own doing; it is the gift of God— not the result of works, so that no one may boast. For we are what he has made us, created in Christ Jesus for good works, which God prepared beforehand to be our way of life."[70] The pri-

---

63. Clark and Dorward, *Walter Hilton: The Scale of Perfection*, 38.
64. Clark and Dorward, *Walter Hilton: The Scale of Perfection*, 79.
65. Levy, *Introducing Medieval Biblical Interpretation*, 137–49.
66. Clark and Dorward, *Walter Hilton: The Scale of Perfection*, 79.
67. Matt 22:36–30
68. Clark and Dorward, *Walter Hilton: The Scale of Perfection*, 280.
69. Thornton, *English Spirituality*, 72–73.
70. Eph 2:8–10.

macy of God. The primacy of the Holy Spirit's role in shaping human hearts and lives toward Christlikeness is fundamental to a proper understanding of the mystics, especially when appropriating their teachings for Christian faith and practice today. The method of practical spiritual theology shares this essential conviction that all growth in the spiritual life is only possible by grace.

SELECT TEACHINGS

Breaking Off

In providing guidance to lay people who might pursue the mixed life, Hilton encourages them to give proper attention to both the active and contemplative aspects of their lives. "If you have been at prayer for some period of time, break off . . . and occupy yourself cheerfully and busily in some physical work for the benefit of your fellow Christians . . . By the same token, when you have for a season been outwardly busy with your employees or other men in pursuit of profit, you should break off and revert to your prayers and devotions."[71]

Contemporary Christians can adopt this pattern of breaking off from active work to contemplative practice and vice versa with great benefit. This "back and forth" pattern between active engagement and contemplative withdrawal may be a particularly helpful practice for scholars, lay and ordained ministers, spiritual directors, and educators. This pattern writ large is the mixed life. It was Hilton's manner of life as an Augustinian canon. Hilton conceived of the mixed life as an option for laypeople with significant responsibilities in the world who still desired to pursue a serious spiritual life.

Every Christian, even the majority who live some form of the active life, will benefit from times of contemplative withdrawal. The inverse of this teaching is also an encouragement. The duties, responsibilities, and relationships people have with others are not to be disregarded for so-called "spiritual things" but attended to faithfully as part of living a spiritual life.[72]

---

71. Jeffery, *Toward a Perfect Love*, 16.
72. Harrison, *Liturgy of the Ordinary*.

Kindling the Fire of Love

A desire for God and for reformation in feeling must be nurtured. Hilton conceives of spiritual practices (what he refers to sometimes as customs) as kindling sticks, to maintain and grow an individual's desire for God. He writes, "The more sticks are laid on a fire, the greater is the flame, and so the more varied the spiritual work that anyone has in mind for keeping his desire whole, the more powerful and ardent shall be his desire for God."[73] Kindling wood is useful in so much as it lights a fire. Hilton argues the same for spiritual practices, "A particular custom is always good to keep if it consists in getting virtue and hindering sin" whereas a custom that "that hinders a better work should be left."[74] Once again, the spiritual life is ultimately relational, a reformation in feeling. Duties and obligations alone are not sufficient for attending to the love of God. Hilton, in keeping with Biblical and Augustinian tradition, conceives of God as a fire, "This is, of course, not to say that God is the element called fire . . . Rather, it is another way of saying that God is love, for just as a fire consumes every physical thing that is combustible, just so the love of God burns and consumes all sin and dross from the soul, refining and purifying it, like an intense fire purifying metal."

Contemporary Christians would do well to attend to their own soul fires. To regularly engage in spiritual practices that keep the fire of their own love for God and neighbor burning bright. This means that ordinarily, if Christians attend to the fire of their faith, they can rely on their faith being a source of strength and consolation. This does not mean there will be no periods of dryness, struggle, or discouragement. It means that as a rule of thumb, the consolations of faith can be more or less regular if the fire of faith is maintained. One of the best things Christian workers of all kinds can do for the people they serve is to attend to the fire of their own faith. This is essential for all spiritual formation. If those responsible for formation find the fires of own their faith barely burning, it will be difficult for them to kindle the flame of faith in others.

---

73. Clark and Dorward, *Walter Hilton: The Scale of Perfection*, 230.
74. Clark and Dorward, *Walter Hilton: The Scale of Perfection*, 230.

The Parable of the Pilgrim

Hilton uses a parable to illustrate the goal and challenges of the spiritual life. In the parable, a pilgrim is told that getting to Jerusalem is difficult, "The way was long and imperiled by hordes of thieves and robbers, as well as many other hindrances such as can beset a traveler. And there was a great diversity of routes . . . along which people were killed and despoiled every day and prevented them from coming to their destination."[75] Yet, the pilgrim is as assured that should he follow one road, he will arrive in the holy city. Pilgrimage to sacred places in order to facilitate spiritual growth was a well-known practice in the time of Hilton and throughout Christian history.[76] The pilgrim is encouraged to remain fixed on the destination. To retain a singular focus on arriving in the city, of ignoring all distractions and temptations, and constantly keeping the purpose of the journey in mind. Hilton writes, "Think always on Jerusalem."[77] Jerusalem represents union with God and "the spiritual presence of Jesus."[78] Hilton commends spiritual exercise to sustain an individual's desire for Jerusalem or God, recognizing that these exercises may vary over time, "For while your desire and the yearning of your heart toward Jesus should be fixed and unchanging, your spiritual endeavors that support you in prayer and in thought, feeling, and nourishing your desire may be diverse and usefully interchanged as you are led by grace in the application to them of your own heart."[79]

Contemporary Christians can benefit from the knowledge that sometimes the spiritual life is arduous. A journey with pitfalls and temptations requiring serious prayer, spiritual exercise, and the grace of God to endure. Without expectation and preparation for such arduous seasons, many Christians may give up hope of arriving at Jerusalem. Lay and ordained ministers, spiritual directors, and educators can help people endure these arduous times through their compassionate presence. Also, as appropriate, they can help prepare others for these seasons of life. Preparation can

---

75. Jeffery, *Toward a Perfect Love*, 105.

76. For a historical literary perspective on pilgrimage: See Chaucer, *The Canterbury Tales*. For Biblical and historical perspectives on pilgrimages as sides to the teaching of the Christian faith, see Smith and Felch, *Teaching and Christian Imagination*, 13–88. Pilgrimage to Jerusalem has shaped Christian understandings of all pilgrimages, both physical and spiritual. See Hillman and Tingle, *Soul Travel*, 6–29.

77. Jeffery, *Toward a Perfect Love*, 106.

78. Jeffery, *Toward a Perfect Love*, 106.

79. Jeffery, *Toward a Perfect Love*, 109.

involve guiding individuals and communities in the intellectual and emotional work surrounding issues of pain and suffering. The ways in which people wrestle in mind and heart when considering the existence of evil and the existence of a God of goodness. In theology, this is referred to as theodicy.[80] Preparation can also involve helping people to find support systems and ways of prayer, new and familiar, that can sustain their desire for God during arduous times. Finally, preparation can involve helping people keep "Jerusalem" in mind. These are some ways an individual or community can assist others in persevering in the spiritual life when the journey becomes arduous.

The Hound and the Hare

Hilton writes, "A hound that runs after the hare, only because he sees other hounds running will rest when he is tired, and turn back; but if he runs because he sees the hare, he will not flag for weariness until he has it."[81] Hilton explains, "If anyone has a grace, however small, and decides to stop working with it and make himself labor at another that he does not yet have, only because he sees or hears that others are doing so, he may indeed run for a while until he is weary; and then he will turn home again." Hilton refers to St. Paul and the spiritual gifts in explaining this illustration.[82] He is encouraging his readers to make use of the gifts and aptitudes that are theirs and not others. He further explains, "For example, some shall be saved and come to blessedness by bodily actions and by works of mercy, some by great penance; some by sorrow and weeping for their sins . . . some by preaching and teaching; and some by various graces and gifts of devotion."[83] There are diverse ways, based on personal giftedness, responsibility, and life situation that individuals can live out the Christian faith.

Contemporary Christians should identify their own gifts and aptitudes and pursue the spiritual life with these, rather than desiring or wishing gifts and aptitudes that are not their own. This is a further refinement of the question of the state of life: active, contemplative, or mixed. For example, if

---

80. Peckham, *Theodicy of Love*. See also Barnes, *When God Interrupts* and Harrison, *Prayer in the Night*.

81. Clark and Dorward, *Walter Hilton: The Scale of Perfection*, 111.

82. Clark and Dorward, *Walter Hilton: The Scale of Perfection*, 111. See also St. Paul's discussion of the gifts in 1 Cor 12, Rom 12, and Eph 4.

83. Clark and Dorward, *Walter Hilton: The Scale of Perfection*, 112.

one is called to the active life and marriage, one should not despair or feel guilty that one cannot live like a contemplative nun spending several hours a day in prayer.

Also, some Christians may be unsure of the goal of their Christian life. It may not be clear to them that there is any rabbit to be chasing. They may only be aware of the other hounds in the pack. If there is no rabbit, no goal for a Christian, they will probably become tired of running with the other hounds, turn away from the chase, or start following the wrong rabbit into a thicket full of thorns. There are a number of implications in this parable for spiritual formation.

The Garden of the Soul

Hilton compares the soul to a garden. Gardening one's soul, cultivating flowers of virtue, and pruning one's sins, naturally flow from this association.[84] However, Hilton's emphasis in this parable is addressing underlying issues. He writes, "In this you could be like a man who had in his garden a polluted well with many irrigation ditches running from it. He went and damned up the ditches, but left the wellspring intact, imagining his problem was solved."[85] Without attention to the sources of various problems of the spiritual life, real progress will be hindered. Hilton writes, "It can be the same way for you and me, even if we have had the grace and strength to stop up our external ditches, failing to beware properly the source within . . . unless you stop and cleanse that as much as you are able, it will corrupt all the flowers in the garden of your soul."[86]

Contemporary Christians will benefit from considering the sources of their problems, especially as they relate to the spiritual life. Why can't I pray? Why have my efforts to practice my faith been less successful than I wished? Why does our congregation feel stuck? Spiritual directors and pastors can help others to explore these questions. Sometimes it can take a long time for an individual, family, or congregation to discover that the issues they are facing have their origin in a hidden source. This is not always the case but looking at the wellsprings of what "waters" a person, family, or congregation can be helpful discernment exercises. Sometimes the garden

---

84. Smith and Felch, *Teaching and Christian Imagination*, 89–137.
85. Jeffery, *Toward a Perfect Love*, 82.
86. Jeffery, *Toward a Perfect Love*, 72.

is being kept perfectly, all is being done appropriately, it is the water that is the issue.

Running After Butterflies

Hilton often enjoins his readers to keep their sights set on the final goal of the spiritual life— union with God. At times he describes this union or realized contemplation, with heaven, sometimes with the vision of Jesus, and at others in arriving in Jerusalem. He describes heaven,

> As great happiness is there, and what wonderful joy and delight; for there is neither sin, nor sorrow, nor passion nor pain, hunger nor thirst, aches nor sickness, doubt nor fear, shame nor blame, nor want of power, nor strength, nor lack of light, nor coldness in love; but there is most excellent beauty, clearness, strength, health, everlasting delights, perfect wisdom, love, peace, honour, security, rest, joy, and bliss in abundance without ever having an end.[87]

There are many distractions from this vision. Hilton writes, "Many . . . are covetous of worldly goods, honours, and . . . riches . . . surely . . . these are not wise; they are like to children that run after butterflies, and, because they look not to their feet, they sometimes easily fall down and break their legs."[88] Hilton wishes his readers to keep focused on the higher aims of the spiritual life.

Contemporary Christians can avoid injury for themselves and others by regularly glancing at the ground of their spiritual feet. This does not mean ignoring earthly matters and everyday responsibilities. It is a warning not to be so distracted by something, however lovely, that one risks injury to themselves. That injury could be physical, emotional, or spiritual. A butterfly may not be a distraction at all. Yet, a child cannot safely follow every butterfly they see, especially if the child never looks to the ground in front of them. It is the same for all spiritual seekers. Hilton is concerned that Christians will allow a butterfly to get them off course from their life in Christ. One butterfly may seem a small concern. Yet, the world is full of butterflies and the ground covering the world full of stumbling blocks.

---

87. Plantinga, *Walter Hilton: Treatise Written to a Devout Man*, 29.
88. Plantinga, *Walter Hilton: Treatise Written to a Devout Man*, 3.

The Courtship of the Soul

Hilton always characterizes both the ends and the means of the spiritual life as being about love. Sometimes Hilton describes God's love in courtly terms.[89] He writes, "The Scriptures are nothing else but love letters, epistles between a loving soul and Jesus its beloved, or as I shall say more truly, between Jesus the true lover and the souls loved by him."[90] For those who have lost a desire for devotion, he recommends, "Concentrate all your desires and activities on preparing a place and a secret chamber in your soul for your Lord Jesus Christ, your husband."[91] This chamber is one of continued devotion, despite a lack of desire for devotion, and a continued practice of prayer, despite a desire to pray. He assures his reader that God in Christ is the wisest of lovers, "Rest assured that all the work that Jesus does in the soul is to make it a true and perfect bride for himself in the height and fullness of love . . . he offers such gracious whispers in the manner of one who is courting, wooing his chosen soul to himself."[92]

Contemporary Christians can benefit from engaging with Holy Scripture as a collection of "love letters." Letters sent from God to themselves. Some will need to shift from a highly historical-analytic reading of Scripture to a more imaginative and contemplative one. A form of the ancient way of meditating on Scripture, called *Lectio Divina* or Sacred Reading,[93] was a practice recommended by Hilton.[94] Most methods of Bible study can be useful but may not on their own facilitate growth in desire for or progress toward union with God. While the bridal and nuptial imagery of courtship will not appeal to all Christians it is a reminder of the relational nature of the spiritual life.

A reminder that in the journey of faith, God is coming from the other direction. God is seeking the human being even more than the human being is seeking God. This relates to the idea of preparing a place for God to visit. Preparing oneself to welcome God at the door of one's heart. Christian

---

89. Courtly terms, including nuptial imagery, and the concept of spiritual marriage were popular themes and illustrations by a wide variety of mystical writers prior to, during, and after Hilton's time. See McGinn, *The Varieties of Vernacular Mysticism*, 332–33, 388.

90. Jeffery, *Toward a Perfect Love*, 169.

91. Walter Hilton, *8 Chapters on Perfection & Angel's Song*, 8.

92. Jeffery, *Toward a Perfect Love*, 171.

93. Charles Cummings. *Monastic Practices*, 7–23.

94. Clark and Dorward, *Walter Hilton*, 37–38.

workers can familiarize themselves with meditative, academic, and devotional ways of reading the Bible. Then patiently and carefully they can help the people they serve encounter the Divine Lover in and through the words of Holy Scripture.

The Foundation of Vocal Prayer

Hilton's Augustinian focus on desire and reformation in feeling is not to be confused with a spirituality that is based purely on emotion. Hilton regularly enjoins his readers to fan the flame of their spiritual love through various exercises and practices. Nonetheless, he recognizes that love is an act of the will and that there will be times when a desire for prayer or devotion to God will be weak or absent. In these circumstances, he encourages persistence in vocal prayer, "Hold on then to the recitation of vocal prayers, and not easily break them off; for often it happens that praying with the mouth keeps devotion; and if in such case you ceased from vocal prayer, your devotion would vanish."[95]

Here and elsewhere, he envisions the spiritual life as a cycle, not unlike that of the contemporary practice of sacred reading. There will be periods of vocal prayer, spiritual reading, meditation, and then, when graced and given, contemplation. Contemplation in the technical sense is a gifted awareness of God's presence. This is sometimes called "infused contemplation."[96] This is in distinction to contemplation as a general term for more reflective forms of faith and practice. In the cycle of sacred reading like in the cycle of ongoing prayer, periods of dryness or accide[97] are bound to come. They are overcome or endured through persistence in prayer and through the gift of love. Hilton writes, "and love does even more, for it slays accidie and the idleness of the flesh, making the soul lively and swift for the service of Jesus."[98]

Contemporary Christians would be wise to develop vocal habits of prayer and not to abandon them, but to develop them as foundational habits for the life of faith. Many Christians do not have a personal habit of prayer, vocal or otherwise. Their primary experience of prayer is within gathered worship and in whatever occasional or regular prayers they offer

---

95. Plantinga, *Walter Hilton: Treatise Written to a Devout Man*, 31.
96. Aumann, *Spiritual Theology*, 330.
97. Allen, *Spiritual Theology*, 74.
98. Clark and Dorward, *Walter Hilton: The Scale of Perfection*, 279.

up to God, often related to intercessions, petitions, and sometimes thanksgivings.[99] Before vocal prayer can be an anchor for an individual's spiritual life they have to learn how to pray and cultivate that practice on a regular, ideally, daily basis. There are many ways of praying and of organizing times for prayer.[100] A foundational goal of all spiritual formation efforts should be the development of a regular, reliable, practice of prayer in each and every Christian and those exploring the Christian faith. Vocal prayer in the medieval sense was often a reference to the Church's official liturgical prayer. Liturgical services, such as Morning and Evening Prayer, were prayed by members of religious communities like Hilton's. This is one way that many Christians have maintained a daily practice of prayer over the centuries. Today many Christians, from many denominations, pray a form of this daily prayer, sometimes known as the Liturgy of the Hours or the Daily Office, at home, at work or with a worshipping community of some kind.[101] Hilton regularly prayed the Liturgy of the Hours with others as a member of the Augustinian community in Thurgarton.

HILTON AND PRACTICAL SPIRITUAL THEOLOGY

The goal of practical spiritual theology is to retrieve the wisdom of past Christian mystics in order to resource and inspire the spiritual lives of Christians today. Spiritual theology provides guidance for the spiritual life. By bringing a mystic's writings into conversation with the ideas of contemporary thinkers and the experience of contemporary believers, older forms of spiritual guidance can be refreshed, renewed, and sometimes reconceived. Certain teachings from past mystics will transfer into the present situation with little adjustment. Other teachings will need to be reimagined for the contemporary situation. Some teachings may need to be set aside because they do not have a place in current Christian understandings of the world or of the love of Jesus Christ. Hilton is a good candidate for this way of doing spiritual theology because we have access to a number of his writings, translated from Latin and Middle English. In these writings, Hilton addresses the spiritual life in comprehensive terms, in ways that are applicable to Christians in a number of situations both in the past and the present.

99. "The principal kinds of prayer are adoration, praise, thanksgiving, penitence, oblation, intercession, and petition." *The Book of Common Prayer*, 856.

100. Blythe, *50 Ways to Pray*.

101. Phyllis Tickle, *The Divine Hours Volumes One, Two, Three*.

Chapter 3

HILTON AND GROOME
A Dialogical Analysis

PHILOSOPHICAL AND THEOLOGICAL UNDERPINNINGS

Retrieving the wisdom of a historical mystic for the present faith and practice of Christians requires engagement with contemporary thinkers and ideas. This can be done in a variety of ways, including using theological and sociological reflection. In this chapter, the ideas of Thomas Groome, a Christian educator and theologian, and the research of Nancy Ammerman, a sociologist of religion, will be brought into dialogue with the theology and practice of fourteenth-century English mystic Walter Hilton. This is one example of a practical spiritual theological method. The theological approach and method of this book. This analysis will highlight the differences between Hilton's ideas and contemporary ideas. It will also suggest potential gaps in Hilton's understanding from a contemporary point of view. Identifying contemporary concerns that are not addressed by a mystic can suggest ways in which the mystic's teachings might be reformulated for current faith and practice.

  This chapter may reveal to practitioners of spiritual formation some of the theoretical and philosophical concerns that sometimes occupy scholars of theology, formation, and education. These philosophical concerns often influence how lay and ordained ministers, spiritual directors, and educators approach their work. All practice, including ministry practice, is shaped by theory, and all theory is shaped by practice.[1] This analysis will also sug-

---

1. Browning, *A Fundamental Practical Theology*, 9.

gest how contemporary methods can be used in the retrieval of Walter Hilton's ideas and counsel. This dialogical approach will also suggest new formulations of Hilton's ideas. In other words, new expressions of spiritual theology. New spiritual theologies rooted in Hilton's medieval ideas and experience but transformed by contemporary ideas and experience. An example of this kind of synthesis, the concept of a "mystic dimension" in Christian education, will be explored. The development of new or refreshed spiritual theologies is a goal of practical spiritual theology. This analysis will begin with an overview of Thomas Groome's understanding of Christian education.

THOMAS GROOME AND THE PURPOSES OF CHRISTIAN EDUCATION

Groome is a helpful conversation partner in the development of practical spiritual theology. His work is comprehensive, addressing pragmatic aspects of religious education, but also philosophical and theological aspects of the same. Religious education, specifically Christian education (also referred to as Christian formation), is a subdiscipline of practical theology.[2] This reflects practical spiritual theology's use of elements of both spiritual theology and practical theology. Thomas Groome's writing on his method of shared praxis provides a comprehensive approach to modern religious education and pastoral ministry.[3] Groome brings his own experience of Christian education with modern persons to his work, as well as reflection on the work of previous thinkers and researchers. Groome's method of *shared Christian praxis* can be used to present a historical writer on the Christian spiritual life to contemporary Christians. This has practical spiritual theological application. Groome writes to instruct communities, teachers of Christian formation, and individual Christian educators.[4]

Groome understands religious education as constituting three essential characteristics: the transcendent, the ontological, and the political.[5] These three characteristics form a foundation for Groome's understanding of formation. The religious character of Christian education is concerned

---

2. See Carol Lakey Hess in chapter 23 on "Religious Education" in Miller-McLemore, *The Wiley-Blackwell Companion to Practical Theology*.

3. Groome, *Sharing Faith*.

4. Groome, *Sharing Faith*, 2–3.

5. Groome, *Sharing Faith*, 11.

with transcendent realities—such as God. In a Christian context, education is intended to foster a relationship with God and others. Christian education is not only concerned with the cognitive dimension of being human, but with every dimension of being human.[6] Groome writes, "'Faith' for Jesus has a power-packed triple demand—beliefs, relationships and commitments—all rolled into a single way of life."[7] The nature of existence or what constitutes being human concerns religious education. This necessarily has a social dimension. Christian education is also political. It is political in the general sense of how knowledge and its exercise can enable or inhibit the flourishing of human communities. It is not necessarily partisan advocating the agenda of a particular party. The content of Christian action, and its nurture of being in relationship with God, others, and self, is not a purely private affair. All instruction has a political or social element.

Building on these three foundational characteristics, Groome outlines three purposes of Christian education. These purposes guide, shape, and inform the practice of and the desired outcomes of all Christian education. The first purpose of Christian education is for the reign of God. The second is for the lived Christian faith. The third is for the wholeness of human freedom for all.[8] These three purposes align with practical spiritual theology's goal to resource and inspire the spiritual lives of Christians today. In other words, retrieving the wisdom and teachings of a past mystic is done principally to support and encourage "lived Christian faith." Groome writes, "I propose the Biblical symbol that best expresses the overarching telos of being Christian and thus evokes the purposes of Christian religious education is the *reign of God*."[9] This concept is derived from Jesus' teaching on the Kingdom of God in the New Testament.[10] Some writers, like Groome, use the word "reign" instead of kingdom.[11] The reign of God points to God's

---

6. Many theories and models of Christian education and spiritual formation affirm the need for a holistic vision of learning. See Anthony, *Christian Education*. See also Chandler, *Christian Spiritual Formation*.

7. Groome, *Will There Be Faith?*, 26.

8. Groome, *Will There Be Faith?*, 14.

9. Groome, *Will There Be Faith?*, 14.

10. Matt 6:33. See also N.T. Wright, *Jesus and the Victory of God*, 198–476. See also Gutierrez, *A Theology of Liberation*.

11. Groome, *Will There Be Faith?*, 14. Groom writes, "From a feminist perspective '*King*dom' of God appears patriarchal. This is one of two reasons I favor the word *reign*; the other is that "reign" is a more accurate translation of the Hebrew *malkuth Yahweh* and the Greek *basileia tou theou*, which refer to an act of reigning rather than to a particular

sovereignty over creation and history. The reign of God contrasts with the reign of many human structures, particularly in its intentions for peace and justice. Human beings can participate in the reign of God, but its completion and realization require God's grace.

Jesus through his life and teaching, death, and resurrection is the central figure of this reign. Practical spiritual theology is also an explicitly Christian theological approach. An approach rooted in the life and teachings, as well as the death and resurrection of Jesus Christ. The reign of God forms the background and ultimate purpose of Christian education for Groome. The more immediate purpose of Christian education is "to promote lived Christian faith in the lives of participants."[12] This lived faith is holistic, engaging the whole person and their social setting. It has cognitive, affective, and behavioral dimensions. Groome critiques the idea, endemic to Western religious education, that imparting cognitive knowledge is sufficient to encourage lived Christian faith. He writes, "Religious education for lived Christian faith is an ontological enterprise that is to inform, form, and transform people in heads, hearts, and life-styles."[13] Groome's third purpose, regarding wholeness and human freedom, affirms traditional ideas of salvation cast in a contemporary idiom, which captures the reality of salvation's consequences for the existential moment and the ultimate hereafter. For Groome, salvation must necessarily have implications for life now, for individuals and communities, and implications for life hereafter. A critique of many mystical writers is their lack of engagement with social concerns. Much of contemporary theology, especially practical theology, is directed toward social concerns. Groome's holistic approach to lived faith includes both personal elements of faith and spirituality and corporate elements of the same.

Groome writes, "My contention is that both the impetus for and the consequence of people living in Christian faith is the wholeness of human freedom that is fullness of life for all, here and hereafter."[14] This broader sense of salvation reflects Groome's concern that Christian education and lived Christian faith will lead to emancipatory ends for all people. Emancipatory means ways in which those who have been marginalized in the Church and the wider society might be given greater freedom, dignity, and

---

realm or domain."

12. Groome, *Will There Be Faith?*, 18.
13. Groome, *Will There Be Faith?*, 18.
14. Groome, *Will There Be Faith?*, 22.

agency.[15] This broader, more holistic concern for education, reflects the concerns intended by the use of the term formation instead of education by many Christian teachers. Educator and activist Parker Palmer writes that "education forms—or deforms—our seeing and our being."[16] Education for Groome is to form and transform individuals. This is also the purpose of practical spiritual theology. Historic mystics are studied not principally for information about the past, but to resource and inspire transformation in the lives of Christians in the present. Transformation for individuals who can then impact communities and the world. Communities that transform individuals who then impact other communities and the world. For Groome, the intended outcome of Christian education is summarized by the word *conation*.

CONATION

Groome has taken the word conation, which is defined as "the conscious drive to perform volitional acts,"[17] and developed its meaning for the purposes of his work. Groome suggests wisdom, in the sense of Christian wisdom, as being an alternative descriptor of conation. He traces the word back to Platonic usage, where conation is "not one of activity of the psyche but the more holistic capacity and disposition people have to realize their own being. It is the agency that undergirds one's cognition, affection, and volition."[18] Conation has to do with the ability people have to realize their own identity and ability to act in the world. Conative activities are activities that engage people holistically, at every level of their being. In other words, such activities are formational activities. Congregants, spiritual directees, and participants in religious education classes are to receive more than information. They are supported in transformation that leads to lived Christian faith. Such activities engage and encourage lived Christian faith holistically, that is cognitively, affectively, and behaviorally.[19]

---

15. Harris, *Fashion Me a People*, 68.
16. Palmer, *To Know as We Are Known*, xxv.
17. Groome, *Sharing Faith*, 26.
18. Groome, *Sharing Faith*, 27.
19. A vision for and attention to the details of a holistic nature of Christian education leading toward transformation is outlined in the writings of John Westerhoff. See especially: Westerhoff, *Will Our Children Have Faith?*

Groome cites the answer to the catechism question, "Why did God make you?" as conative, "to know, love, and serve God in this life."[20] Christian education should be conative and conative educative activity should lead to Christian wisdom. Groome contrasts wisdom with a narrow educative focus on reason. Wisdom includes reason but exceeds it. Groome writes that "wisdom's major features are 'reflectiveness' and 'sound judgment' regarding the 'the means and ends of practical life.'"[21] Wisdom about the ways of God. Wisdom about the ways of life that are most life giving. Wisdom about the ways of the Holy Spirit. Wisdom is preeminently embodied in Jesus Christ, whom the Scriptures declare as being "the wisdom of God."[22] Mystics then are bearers of wisdom, in a derivative sense based on their own experience with God and others. God is the fire. The source of wisdom. The mystics are the masters of spiritual kindling, of setting the conditions in themselves and others for spiritual sparks to fly. The sparks of the Holy Spirit that set their lives and the lives of others on fire with the love of God. Practical spiritual theology is a process intended in the proverbial sense of the wisdom literature of the Old Testament to sharpen iron upon iron.[23] The analogy of education is a social process—a process of shared growth. The "iron" of the witness and writings of a past Christian mystic sharpen the "iron" of present Christian faith and practice. By the power of the Holy Spirit, the writings of the mystics still smolder. There is still heat in the metaphorical coals of their words. Attending to their words can be a means of igniting their writings into flames that fuel contemporary lived Christian faith. Groome's method of shared Christian praxis can help facilitate this process of kindling.

EPISTEMOLOGY: BEYOND COGNITIVE KNOWLEDGE

Cognitive knowledge is recognized as one aspect of knowing and is connected to the more holistic notion of being. Groome's approach, while valuing the contributions of critical rationality, argues for a phenomenological and liberating approach to knowledge.[24] In other words, Groome includes rational approaches to knowledge acquisition as a valid and

---

20. Groome, *Sharing Faith*, 30.
21. Groome, *Sharing Faith*, 32.
22. 1 Cor 1:24.
23. Prov 27:17. "Iron sharpens iron, and one person sharpens the wits of another."
24. Groome, *Sharing Faith*, 74, 80.

necessary part of Christian education. He also includes other ways of knowing and experiencing the world in his approach to Christian education. This liberating approach means that any evaluation of formation efforts should not be limited to the acquisition of facts and concepts. For example, did people learn about the freedom of God in today's Bible study on Exodus? Evaluation of formational efforts should include considerations of lived Christian faith. For example, are people in the Bible study starting to live with more freedom? Are they supporting the freedom of others, especially those who face obstacles, social, political, or otherwise in living freely? This same holistic approach is taken in practical spiritual theology. The goal is not for participants to know some facts about a mystic but for them to live out their faith in familiar, fresh, and increasingly faithful ways. Ways that bring blessings to themselves and others.

Groome affirms much of traditional theology and formational approaches. This is important in building a bridge between the traditional theology of a mystic, in this case, Hilton, and the contemporary situation. However, Groome also critiques traditional theology. Critique is an important part of practical theology as an academic discipline. He identifies four critical areas of significance.

These four areas are also significant for the work of practical spiritual theology. The first is that critical approaches or post-enlightenment reason have brought about the recognition of the historically conditioned nature of Christian faith, symbols, and theology. Mystical teachings did not arise in a vacuum, they must be situated in a particular place and time. The second area is the development of critical biblical scholarship, which has brought more constructive and deconstructive views to Scripture texts. Mystical writings can be studied through the whole range of scholarly approaches to interpretation and hermeneutics. The third area is that critical approaches have encouraged the reformulation of Christian ideas in dialectic with numerous social situations and settings. A potential outcome of a practical spiritual theological method is the reformulation of a mystic's teachings in ways that relate to specific social settings. The fourth area is personal reflexivity, which calls for educators and interpreters to recognize their socially conditioned assumptions and interests. The researcher brings their own assumptions and perspectives to the study of a given mystic. These assumptions and perspectives should be acknowledged rather than blindly held. [25] Finally, to summarize, Groome argues for what he calls a "human-

---

25. Groome, *Sharing Faith*, 81.

izing rationality that brings knowers and known into a dialectical and right relationship of care that is life-giving for self, others, and creation."[26] This holistic vision compliments the pursuit of holiness, which is another way of speaking of human wholeness.[27]

SHARED CHRISTIAN PRAXIS

In order to achieve the ends of Christian education, Groome proposes a pedagogical method of shared Christian praxis. A way of engaging learners. He writes, "Praxis as the defining term of this pedagogical approach refers to the consciousness and agency that arise from and are expressed in any and every aspect of people's being as agent-subjects-in-relationship whether realized in actions that are personal, interpersonal, sociopolitical, or cosmic."[28] The approach is shared. It is a method of theological presentation and reflection. The educator or presenter engages in the learning process with others. It is not a banking model of education.[29] The Christian part of this model is specifically the Christian story and vision, which broadly speaking, "includes God's self-disclosure to the people of Israel as mediated through the Hebrew Scriptures; it has its highpoint in Jesus the Christ, who Christians believe is the heart of God's Story and Vision for humankind; and it symbolizes the Christian tradition since then and the living faith to which disciples are called in the community of Jesus."[30] The mystic, their story and writings, become the example of the Christian story and vision in a practical spiritual theological approach. The use of the word "story" implies people, life, and the embodied ends of Christian education. For Groome, story encompasses doctrinal truth and connotes a wider meaning appropriate for the broader ends of conation. There are five movements to Groome's model of shared Christian praxis. A focusing or gathering activity precedes the five movements. The movements are: (1) Naming Present Praxis, (2) Critical Reflection on Present Praxis, (3) Making Accessible Christian Story and Vision, (4) Dialectical Hermeneutic to Appropriate the Christian Story and Vision to Participants' Stories and

---

26. Groome, *Sharing Faith*, 82.
27. Merton, *Emblems of a Season of Fury*, 61–69. See also Palmer, *A Hidden Wholeness*.
28. Groome, *Sharing Faith*, 136.
29. Freire, *Pedagogy of the Oppressed*, 54.
30. Groome, *Sharing Faith*, 139.

Visions, and (5) Decision/Response for Lived Christian Faith.[31] This model can be used as part of the work of practical spiritual theology with any number of historical mystics, Hilton is just one example.

HILTON AND SHARED CHRISTIAN PRAXIS: AN EXAMPLE

To explore how Groome's model of shared Christian praxis might be employed, a hypothetical case study will be utilized using the five movements of his model. The purpose of this thought exercise is to illustrate one possible form of practical spiritual theological method. In keeping with the aims of practical spiritual theology, this imagined case study will also use sociological data. In this case, the data serves as a check and balance to the speculative nature of this exercise. Sociological data can also enrich theological reflections with actual groups of people. In this imagined study, sociological research will help participants identify themselves in relation to the spiritual perspectives of others. The imagined setting of this case study will be a morning of reflection at a local church with participants drawn from a local university. The participants are a mixture of undergraduate and graduate students. The initial focusing activity is a brief presentation of Walter Hilton, following the major contours of the information provided earlier in this work. The participants are given an opportunity to respond to this presentation and ask further questions about Hilton. This lays an initial foundation for their engagement with Hilton that will be further explored in movement three.

MI: Exploring Spirituality

The first movement involves a general brainstorming and discussion revolving around the question, "What is spirituality?" This is the focusing activity. It helps the participants to begin the process of engaging with the presentation. It involves brainstorming as many ideas—freely associated—with spirituality. The ideas might be displayed to the gathering on a board or through technological means. There is no judgment of ideas by the presenter, all ideas are recorded. The second part of this movement, an exploration of spirituality, involves grouping the brainstormed ideas together

---

31. Groome, *Sharing Faith*, 146–48.

and looking for common themes to develop and emerge. Ideas and themes of prayer, God, meditation, and other activities and concepts are presented by the group. The issue of identity also emerges. That is the discussion of the question of religion versus spirituality. Some students identify with or sympathize with the idea of being spiritual but not religious.[32]

M2: Critical Reflection on Spirituality

The second movement features the research of Nancy Ammerman as a conversation partner to deepen participants' understanding of the contemporary landscape of spirituality. It also helps participants articulate their own sense of spirituality. Ammerman's research is helpful because students participating in the morning of reflection come from across the United States and Canada. Her research would not be appropriate if a similar day of reflection were being conducted in the United Kingdom. In that situation, sociological data and research done in the British context would be needed. Ammerman's extensive qualitative research of American spirituality resulted in the identification of three major spiritual tribes across the population: *theistic*, *extra-theistic*, and *ethical*. Theistic spirituality is linked to the divine, while extra-theistic locates spirituality in various naturalistic forms of transcendence, and ethical spirituality focuses on everyday compassion.[33] Students in the morning of reflection are encouraged to consider which tribe best describes their own sense of spiritual identity, as each is described in greater depth.

The theistic tribe sees spirituality as being linked with God, particular practices, as well as with "mysterious encounters" with God or the divine in daily life. Ammerman describes this tribe as having the ability to "see events as both ordinary and extraordinary, material and spiritual."[34] Theistic spirituality was strongly associated with those involved in congregations, and less so with those without any affiliation. This was the largest tribe and it also reflected that "a large portion of our American sample is spiritually religious and religiously spiritual."[35]

The extra-theistic tribe understands life as having a larger meaning. This meaning is an "immanent frame of explainability and calculation is

32. See White, *The Rise of the Nones*.
33. Ammerman, *Sacred Stories*, 19.
34. Ammerman, *Sacred Stories*, 29.
35. Ammerman, *Sacred Stories*, 31.

opened to something beyond . . . what they are describing may not come from a transcendent deity, but it is nevertheless transcendent."[36] This tribe might be described as embodying a spirituality of awe, of "what one feels."[37] The icon of this tribe, "the solitary, contemplating person has become the icon of American spirituality, and this sort of spiritual experience the essence of authentic religiosity."[38] The research revealed that the nonreligious, "if they have any spiritual vocabulary at all, are likely to speak of it as meaning, awe, connection, and inner wisdom."[39]

The ethical tribe highlights one aspect of spirituality that all of Ammerman's spiritual tribes agreed upon, "that real spirituality is about living a virtuous life, one characterized by helping others, transcending one's own selfish interests to seek what is right."[40] This tribe could include people who have a different understanding of the value of believing. It could "either be a way of talking about devout spirituality or a way of describing superstition."[41] One interesting theme for those in this category, and the larger category of non-religious, was an experience they usually had in college. It would be interesting to hear from the student participants about their current experience related to the following findings in Ammerman's research: "One theme in the secular stories was an encounter with knowledge, usually during their college years, that challenged the beliefs they were taught. Since belief was seen as central to what religion and spirituality are, the implausibility of religious beliefs was a critical factor in their exodus from both."[42] This finding of the study, as well as others, has many implications for the work of spiritual formation.

Ammerman's research revealed that "most of our participants inhabit both spiritual and religious spaces at the same time."[43] Her research revealed that the "spiritual but not religious" label was more of "a boundary-maintaining device and source of legitimacy than as a description of the empirical situation."[44] In other words it was difficult to identify what actual

36. Ammerman, *Sacred Stories*, 35.
37. Ammerman, *Sacred Stories*, 29.
38. Ammerman, *Sacred Stories*, 31.
39. Ammerman, *Sacred Stories*, 35.
40. Ammerman, *Sacred Stories*, 35.
41. Ammerman, *Sacred Stories*, 40.
42. Ammerman, *Sacred Stories*, 41.
43. Ammerman, *Sacred Stories*, 41.
44. Ammerman, *Sacred Stories*, 51.

spiritual practices characterized this group. In some ways, the designation, "spiritual, not religious" served as a placeholder. Ammerman writes, "people are equating 'religion' to the implausible beliefs and discredited institutions they have rejected. They are claiming 'spirituality' as a reasonably positive and generic category and one that each individual can fill with the content of her own choosing."[45] Since most of the participants in Ammerman's research expressed some sense of spirituality as a positive force (i.e., the theistic and extra-theistic tribes), it is likely that a medieval mystic like Hilton might be of interest to many twenty-first century North Americans as they seek to understand and live out their own spirituality.

M3: Hilton as a Vision of Spirituality

In this third movement, Hilton is presented as an embodiment of the Christian story and vision in a particular place and time. At this point, participants have discussed spirituality in general and considered their own spiritual identity in light of Ammerman's research. Hilton is then presented as an example of Christian spirituality. The basic facts of his life are reviewed, as well as the major themes from his writings. Some of his teachings and recommendations on the spiritual life are shared. In an actual situation, attention would need to be given to what specific information to share about Hilton and what specific teachings. If more than one morning of reflection were held, different ways of presenting Hilton could be utilized and reflected upon. Groome's model could be used in a variety of ways to present Hilton and other mystics with a number of populations and communities.

M4: Dialogue between M2 and M3

Movement four involves a discussion with the students about how Hilton might speak to each of these spiritual tribes as well as themselves directly. Hilton seems to have the most resonance and resourcing potential for those belonging to the theistic tribe. Hilton himself is operating from this perspective. His teachings are intended to help individuals pursue union with God. Further, Ammerman's sample had a largely Christian background, though it included Jewish and Wiccan participants. Hilton's status

---

45. Ammerman, *Sacred Stories*, 51.

as a Christian teacher also recommends him to those embracing a similar belief. The concept of the mixed life has some appeal to those with an extra-theistic spirituality; in that, it would provide a framework for attending to both spiritual growth and practice, and other aspects of life. It is uncertain whether participants in the ethical spiritual tribe find much value in Hilton. This tribe, while the smallest, is composed of those with the least interest in or involvement in any religious community. Some reject him as they have rejected religion in most of its forms. Some see him as valuable only to the extent that those who follow his teachings live an ethical life. Hilton offers a critique and a challenge to those in the extra-theistic and ethical tribes in questioning whether a spiritual life can be pursued by oneself, isolated from a religious and spiritual community. Hilton attempted to do this as a hermit but found that approach lacking.[46]

M5: Steps (Potential Praxis in Contemporary Situation)

The fifth movement involves dialoguing with the students about what steps they need to take, if any, related to their own spiritual development. Related to this question is how, if at all, Hilton might be useful in discerning or taking those steps. The responses to what next steps students take vary considerably. For some, it involves specific spiritual practices. For example, prayer, silence, gratitude, or yoga. For others, it was their involvement with a religious or spiritual community. In an actual and not speculative case study, further opportunities to discuss and study Hilton could be offered to participants. Groome's model of shared Christian praxis offers one way for spiritual practitioners and scholars to engage in the work of practical spiritual theology. While Groome's method can be used speculatively, it is designed to be used with people. The emerging method of practical spiritual theology can be used in formal research conducted by scholars and in the more informal, but no less important, ways of an investigation conducted by lay and ordained ministers, spiritual directors, and educators. It is a flexible method.

---

46. A fourteenth-century hermit was still part of medieval society and was specifically seeking a Christian spiritual life, which involved engagement with the Church.

DIALOGICAL HIGHLIGHTS

Walter Hilton and Thomas Groome are separated by seven hundred years. Spiritual theologians from the Middle Ages cannot be expected to demonstrate familiarity with modern forms of scholarship and certain modern questions. Nonetheless, bringing a modern theologian into dialogue with a historical theologian is a fruitful exercise for practical spiritual theology. Hilton and Groome share an orientation toward the transcendent. Hilton's work as a spiritual director is directed toward union with God. Groome's work as an educator includes a transcendent dimension. Both are also concerned with being, but in different ways. Hilton's concern with the ontological is contemplative. He understands, in Augustinian fashion, that human beings are meant to find the ground of their being in God.

Groome also understands the ontological dimension in relational terms, but he is more emphatic about the social dimensions of being and of the Christian faith more widely. He writes, "It would seem patently true, however, that religious education is to make a fundamental difference in how people realize their being in relation with God, self, others, and the world."[47] Hilton's teachings do engage these wider considerations, though mainly in personal terms. For the medieval contemplative, the self is oriented toward God and less toward others. Hilton writes about the third and highest part of contemplation, describing it as, "the knowing and perfect loving of God."[48] For the medieval active, the self is oriented toward God, others, and the world. Hilton comments, "Active life lies in love and charity shown outwardly in good . . . works" and "in the fulfilment of God's commandments."[49] For the individual pursuing the mixed life, it is alternating between the contemplative (God) and the active (others and the world). Groome's orientation toward the political is explicit while Hilton's is implicit. For Hilton, the political dimensions of Christian teaching are embodied in the society he lived in. To live faithfully according to one's state of life is to contribute to the common good of all.[50] Groome offers a critique of the mystical life in his assessment of Neoplatonism's influence on Christianity, "Praxis was disparaged as unreliable and it was overshadowed by the

---

47. Groome, *Sharing Faith*, 11.
48. Clark and Dorward, *Walter Hilton: The Scale of Perfection*, 82.
49. Clark and Dorward, *Walter Hilton: The Scale of Perfection*, 78.
50. The contemplative path was generally recognized as being for a few, not all. The proper ordering of society, from a spiritual perspective, required those in the active and mixed lives to tend to their societal duties and obligations.

contemplative life as a way to perfection."[51] Hilton's insistence that those in the active and mixed states attend to the needs of their neighbor provides a contrast to this criticism.[52]

Hilton and Groome agree on the central thrust of Christian education or spiritual direction as being lived Christian faith. Hilton does not directly engage in significant discussions of the Kingdom of God, or as Groome describes it, the reign of God. The political and structural integration of the Christian faith was more explicit in fourteenth-century England, bringing elements of the reign of God, as Groome describes it, into the everyday lives of Hilton and his contemporaries.[53] While there are many differences in method and philosophy between the two theologians, one of the most significant, in terms of contemporary Christian living, is Groome's third purpose of Christian education: "for the wholeness of human freedom that is fullness of life for all."[54] Groome, throughout his work, stresses the emancipatory and liberating aspects of the Gospel. While Hilton cannot be expected to engage with critical and contextual theologies that arose centuries after his death, he does not engage in any significant discussion of the social problems of his time.

His teachings on charity and love of neighbor indicate he is concerned that Christians in the active and mixed states attend to the needs of others, but, for the most part, he does not explore how they might do this. He is writing to individuals who are seeking direction about their prayer life and how to pursue deeper intimacy with God, whether as an anchoress or as a man of responsibility in the world. Likewise, his contemporaries, such as Julian of Norwich and Richard Rolle, when writing similar works, tend not to discuss social problems. Even Catherine of Siena, another fourteenth-century mystic, whose ministry was politically and socially engaged on many fronts,[55] gives little explicit attention or recommendations concerning social issues in her mystical work, *The Dialogue*.[56] Yet, in her hundreds of letters, she regularly engages the social issues of the day.[57] Perhaps, Hil-

---

51. Groome, *Sharing Faith*, 51.

52. Jeffery, *Toward a Perfect Love*, 9–11.

53. For a more detailed exploration of the role of the Church and State in Hilton's time see Pantin, *The English Church in the Fourteenth Century*.

54. Groome, *Sharing Faith*, 21.

55. Luongo, *The Saintly Politics of Catherine of Siena*.

56. Catherine of Siena, *The Dialogue*.

57. Catherine of Siena, *The Dialogue*, 76.

ton, situated in village life in Thurgarton, did engage in social works or ministry, but we have no record of such.

Groome praises some aspects of Augustine's epistemology, which are evident in Hilton.[58] The first is the Augustinian understanding of the unity of reason, memory, and will. Groome writes, "Augustine, even more than Plato . . . recognized the need for unity between thought and action and for reciprocity between the contemplative life of union with God and the practical life of Christian virtue."[59] The second is Augustine's recognition of the importance of human memory, story, and experience. Augustine is an exemplar of this tradition in his *Confessions*,[60] but this approach is evident in some of his other, more didactic, writings.[61] Hilton sometimes prefaces his comments as coming out of his own experience and he encourages his directees to make adjustments to their spiritual practice based on their own experiences. At the end of the first book of *The Scale*, written to an anchoress, he writes, "So with these words that I write; do not take them too strictly, but where, after thinking them over well, you feel that I speak too shortly— either for lack of English or for want of reason—I beg you to amend it, only where it is necessary." Hilton is aware that his writings are not perfect and he gives the anchoress freedom in understanding how they apply to her situation. Hilton's method of spiritual direction finds common ground with Groome's method of shared Christian praxis.[62] Groome critiques Augustine for his sexism, in associating the mind with men and women with the body.[63] There is not a discernible difference in Hilton's direction to women or men. The differences in direction are almost entirely based on their state in life. For contemplatives, he encourages traditional contemplative life and practices. For those with worldly responsibilities desiring a closer relationship with God, he encourages the practices of the mixed life. We can assume that Hilton was a man of his time and may have shared certain views on women that would no longer be tenable.

58. Groome, *Sharing Faith*, 53.
59. Groome, *Sharing Faith*, 54.
60. Augustine, *Confessions*.
61. Groome, *Sharing Faith*, 54.
62. Groome's general movement from life-to-faith-to-life, is not dissimilar to Hilton's method of referring his directees to their own experience (and sometimes his own or that of others) then back to the teachings of the faith, and then back to their own practice and future experience.
63. Groome, *Sharing Faith*, 55.

Nonetheless, his counsel to women is akin to his counsel to men, and many of the readers of his works were women, both vowed religious and lay.

THE MYSTIC DIMENSION OF CHRISTIAN EDUCATION

According to Groome, lived Christian faith is the purpose and intended outcome of Christian formation and education. This lived Christian faith is about individuals and communities. According to Hilton, union with God is the purpose and intended outcome of the spiritual life. This union with God is individualistic, shared between the lover, God, and the beloved, the mystic. Synthesizing these two purposes together suggests that there should be a "mystic dimension" to all Christian education. Mystic means an experiential encounter with God. Literature and religion scholar Barbara Newman describes mysticism as "a quest for experiential union with God" that "seeks to transcend all categories of human thought."[64]

Author and spiritual director Evelyn Underhill writes, "The Christian mystic therefore is one for whom God and Christ are not merely objects of belief, but living facts experientially known as firsthand."[65] A goal then of Christian formation should be the cultivation of participants' spiritual life. A cultivation with the purpose of helping participants engage with the experience of God and engage with those who have experienced God. Hilton and other mystics remind contemporary believers that awareness of God's presence cannot be forced, it can only be cultivated.

The work of all spiritual formation should be done with this mystic dimension in mind. English scholar and writer Mary Rose O'Reilley writes, "Pedagogy emphasizes technique; spirituality addresses who we are."[66] Walter Hilton identifies the reforming of the image of God in human beings as the central work of the spiritual life.[67] It is the *imago* of God in every human being that makes possible a mystic dimension in all Christian education. Parker Palmer writes, "Through the disciplines of spiritual formation we see to be re-formed in our original, created image."[68] This can be implemented in various settings by engagement with the mystics, teaching spiritual

---

64. Lamm, *Christian Mysticism*.
65. Underhill, *The Mystics of the Church*, 3.
66. O'Reilley, *Radical Presence*, 14.
67. Clark and Dorward, *Walter Hilton: The Scale of Perfection*, 36, 193–99.
68. Palmer, *To Know as We Are Known*, 17.

practices, and developing a culture of openness to the Holy Spirit.[69] Sometimes Christian communities only tangentially give attention to cultivating participants' abilities to pursue the spiritual life and experience the presence of God. Spiritual formation, spiritual direction, and prayer are often seen as the province of a small group of individuals interested in spirituality. How can the mystic dimension of spiritual formation be woven into every aspect of congregational life and into every form of Christian ministry, as well as for all ages? This is a question best answered from within particular communities and settings. However, part of answering this question may involve addressing a concern that some have about mysticism. The concern is that mysticism is only inwardly focused on the self and God and not outwardly focused on the needs of others and the world. A response to that concern is another synthesis, another reformulated expression of spiritual theology based on the dialogical analysis between Groome and Hilton. This concept, *conative mysticism*, is an outflow of the mystic dimension to all spiritual formation.

CONATIVE MYSTICISM

According to Groome, lived Christian faith is a purpose and intended outcome of Christian education and formation. For Hilton, union with God was the goal of the spiritual life. This union transforms the individual, purging them of sin, developing their virtues, and ultimately filling them with the love of God. This is seen as the goal of the contemplative life and the ultimate goal of the Christian life, existentially and eternally. Groome's concept of conation does not exclude this sort of relationship between the self and God but its goals and concerns are broader, "conative activity engages people's corporal, mental, and volitional capacities, their heads, hearts, and overt behaviors, their cognition, desire, and will, as they realize their own being in right relationship with others and the world and contribute in ways that are life giving for all."[70]

A prayerful sense of conation, a sense of drawing together all the aspects of human psychology, is expressed by sixteenth-century century bishop and writer Thomas Cranmer in *The Book of Common Prayer*, "Almighty God, unto whom all hearts are open, all desires known, and from whom no

---

69. For a model and example of developing a local church into a community open to the Holy Spirit, see N. Graham Standish, *Becoming a Blessed Church*.

70. Groome, *Sharing Faith*, 30.

secrets are hid: Cleanse the thoughts of our hearts by the inspiration of thy Holy Spirit, that we may perfectly love thee, and worthily magnify thy holy Name; through Christ our Lord."[71] This prayer brings together the holistic nature of lived Christian faith found in Groome with the mystical elements of cleansing, desiring, and love found in Hilton. This prayer, and the experience behind it, facilitates conative mysticism. The prayer is also one theological description of conative mysticism.

The mystic seeking conation is seeking union with God holistically, in ways that transform themselves and promote the transformation of others and the world. Groome uses the word wisdom as an alternative to conation. Mystic wisdom, in this sense, is not only the experience of the self uniting to God, but the self increasingly becoming wise to the ways of God, in embodied ways that lead to transformation for all. This broader notion of the goal of the spiritual life is present in Hilton's writings as those pursuing the active and mixed lives must attend to the love of their neighbor.

Conative mysticism may be especially suited for those pursuing the mixed life. Further, a contemplative by grace, entering a fully realized conative mysticism, contributes to the welfare of all through their life of prayer. Conative union implies not only union with God, but a unity of spirit between the self, others, and all of creation. This implies, in Hilton's terms, a love of neighbor that by grace has been purged, illuminated, and through union with God, transformed into a selfless love. A love that turns inward on self and God and a love that turns outward toward others and the world. This is a mysticism that can help facilitate in Groome's terms, wholeness and freedom for all. Conative mysticism can commend all of Hilton's teachings while encouraging broader applications of love of neighbor to encompass liberating concerns such as gender and race, which feature prominently in Groome's work.

In other words, conative mysticism is not mere navel-gazing or a private spiritual experience. Rather conative mysticism draws individuals into the heart of God from which they are sent out into the world to love. The beloved, the mystic, grows increasingly in their love for God through the traditional practices of the spiritual life, but they also grow in their love for those things that God loves. Scripture describes these things in many ways, including: "For God so loved the world" and God loves the "least of these."[72] God loves the world. God loves the least of those who are

---

71. *The Book of Common Prayer*, 323.

72. John 3:16; Matt 25:35–40. See Sobrino, *Spirituality of Liberation*, 2. "When all is

cared for or not cared for by God's people. A relationship between deep mystical experience and deep engagement with the world for the sake of God's love is found in the history of Christian mysticism. For example, the fourteenth-century Italian mystic, Catherine of Siena, adds a fourth stage of Christian growth after completive union. A birthing stage. Dominican sister and Catherine scholar Susan Noffke writes, "Filiality in Christ is far more than simply being fathered and mothered by God. Filiality in Christ becomes a commitment, even a passion, to 'continue the lineage' as it were, to give birth to others in God and in Christ."[73] After experiencing union with God, the mystic realizes a deep conation, a deep wisdom in God, and is sent out into the world. Not only does the mystic pursue the reformation of the image of God within themselves, but also for the sake of others. Today this reformation of the image may be understood to have personal dimensions as well as corporate dimensions. Many forms of social injustice deny the *imago* of God, the very humanity, of a group of people in order to justify their mistreatment. Conative mysticism can then be a support for and motivation for the work of restoring the image of God in both social structures and human hearts. This concept, derived from dialogue between and a synthesis of Hilton and Groome, is an example of an outcome of practical spiritual theology.

CONTEMPORARY THINKERS AND IDEAS IN PRACTICAL SPIRITUAL THEOLOGY

The dialogue between a mystic's historical concerns and formulations and a contemporary thinker's concerns and formulations can be revealing. It may reveal differences between the thinkers, including gaps in mystical writings that need to be addressed in light of contemporary Christian concerns. In the case of Walter Hilton and Thomas Groome, the differences suggested a synthesis of their work in the area of mysticism's social dimensions. This resulted in new expressions of spiritual theology to support the faith and practice of Christians today. Namely, the mystic dimension in Christian education and the concept of conative mysticism.

While only partially explored through an speculative case study, the use of social science data can also enhance the understanding of medieval

---

said and done, the spiritual life must be efficacious for the transformation of the secular reality around us, helping us steer that reality in the direction of the reign of God."

73. Noffke, *Catherine of Siena*, 69.

mystics by contemporary audiences. Whereas Groome may be an ongoing conversational partner in the development of practical spiritual theology, Nancy Ammerman's place as a conversation partner in future retrieval projects will be dependent on the research participants involved. Different settings will necessitate the use of relevant research in a given setting. This use of sociological data and philosophical insights from Christian education are ways in which practical spiritual theology can bring the insights of a historic mystic into conversation with the ideas and experiences of contemporary believers. The goal of these methods is to resource and inspire faith and practice today.

Chapter 4

HILTON AND SOUTHWELL CHRISTIANS
A Conversational Analysis

WALTER HILTON AND CONTEMPORARY CHRISTIANS IN SOUTHWELL, ENGLAND

The goal of practical spiritual theology is to do spiritual theology through the writings of a specific mystic and put those writings into conversation with the ideas and experiences of contemporary believers. This method may involve bringing a mystic into dialogue with a contemporary theologian, contemporary sociological research, or in dialogue with contemporary believers. This results in an empirically grounded practical spiritual theology. A spiritual theology rooted in the wisdom of the past, grounded in contemporary ideas and experience, for the purposes of resourcing the faith and practice of Christians in the present. Walter Hilton, this book's case study for this theological method, lived out his entire ministry as an Augustinian Canon at the Augustinian priory in Thurgarton, England. Knowledge of Hilton is limited in the lands of Hilton, as the author discovered during three research trips, taken in three consecutive years to Thurgarton.

The village of Thurgarton remains, including St. Peter's, a small but active Church of England parish, which is on the site of the original medieval priory and includes architecture from Hilton's time. Despite a memorial plaque and image of Hilton on one of the church's pillars, few are familiar with his teachings. To the north, about 6 kilometers (3.7 miles), is the town of Southwell,[1] which includes the historic Minster Church.[2] The Minster was a significant center in the fourteenth century. Hilton likely visited the Minster either occasionally or regularly depending on his duties at the priory church in Thurgarton.[3]

Method and Location of Research

The experience of getting to know the region and the leadership of the Minster in Southwell, including the parish church in Thurgarton, led the author to conduct semi-structured small group interviews in Southwell. Two groups gathered, comprising sixteen persons, women and men, laity, and clergy. These interviews took place during a fourth trip to the region in May 2019. Semi-structured interviews were chosen to emphasize the experience of contemporary Christians in Southwell. Participants volunteered, drawn from the Minster congregation, which includes individuals from across the town and out into the rural areas that extend to Thurgarton and beyond. The responses of participants were kept confidential.[4] The leadership of the Minster, especially the Dean, Canon Theologian, and Retreat House Wardens, helped to facilitate these interviews. They were held at the Sacrista Prebend Retreat House, which is across the street from the Minster. Since the author's first trip, the leadership of the retreat house has been extremely supportive of the research project. One of the rooms, where the author has resided during every trip, is named after Walter Hilton. The plan was to conduct three semi-structured group interviews. No volunteers came to the first scheduled group. However, the second and third groups were well attended.

    1. Southwell is a town of approximately 7000 individuals located in Nottinghamshire County, approximately three hours north of London.
    2. Minster is a term given to certain English Churches with historic monastic foundations. Southwell Minster is also the Cathedral Church for the Anglican Diocese of Southwell and Nottingham.
    3. This is a guess based on the importance and proximity of the Minster (Southwell) and Priory (Thurgarton) in the fourteenth century.
    4. Participants signed a form explaining the research process and confidential measures of the project. Data was collected by the author by note taking as well as audio recording. These recordings were later transcribed, and no data about the names of participants were recorded. All data is stored digitally under password protection. The entire project was reviewed and approved as meeting the ethical protocols and standard research practices with human subjects by the Institutional Review Board of St. Thomas University, Miami, FL, USA, on May 2, 2019.

The approved outline of this research, called a protocol, used semi-structured small group interviews with five movements. The goal was to ensure the exploration of certain topics while keeping the conversation as open-ended and in-depth as possible. It was expected that respondents would provide data on some of these topics without being asked, particularly the sub-questions in the protocol. Standard neutral follow-ups, such as "tell me more," were used wherever applicable. The questions were constructed to move from initial rapport-building questions (that helped put the respondents at ease) to a sequencing of questions. Such sequences were designed to move from the present and toward the past and future, from the impersonal to the personal, and from participants' personal experiences to reflections on the possibilities for others within the wider Church. The data from these interviews were analyzed using theologian John Swinton and researcher Harriet Mowat's qualitative method as well as theologian and priest Jeff Astley's method of doing ordinary theology.[5] These approaches helped to inform the emerging method of practical spiritual theology. The questions in abbreviated form were:

1. When you think of spirituality or mysticism today, what comes to mind?
2. What do you think about the three states of life, starting with the contemplative, but also considering the active and mixed as Hilton described them?
3. As a means to contemplation Hilton recommended the reading of Holy Scripture, meditation, and diligent prayer. How do you imagine these three practices might help people in their relationship with God?
4. Hilton recommended moderation in bodily and spiritual practices, how might they relate to your own faith and spirituality?
5. How might Hilton and his teachings be a help to the spiritual life of Christians today?

---

5. Swinton and Mowat, *Practical Theology and Qualitative Research*. See also Scharen, *Fieldwork in Theology*. In addition to these methods, this research builds upon the work of ordinary theology, listening to the voices of the faithful as serious sources of theological reflection. See Astley, *Ordinary Theology: Looking, Listening, and Learning in Theology*.

CONTEMPORARY CHRISTIAN RESPONSE TO WALTER HILTON

First Movement: Opening

Each semi-structured interview began with a question, worded similarly to, "We've gathered here in the land where Hilton is from, one of the great spiritual teachers of the English mystical tradition, whose insights and teachings may offer something important for our time. Let's begin thinking about spirituality and mysticism in general. When you think of mysticism today, what comes to mind?" Group participants shared a variety of answers: "Sense of God, silence, participating in the being of God, being aware of the influence of the Spirit," and more. More than one individual in each group brought up the idea of "otherworldliness."

Otherworldliness is tied to the idea of there being "something else," something more than the material. One participant expressed it as, "Untouchable, something you can't touch." Another participant stressed the necessity of individuals having an openness to this other reality in order to experience it. When prompted about how individuals could experience this sense of otherworldliness, participants suggested art and nature. One group associated mysticism with particular places, such as "Iona and Northumberland." Several shared experiences of going to retreat centers, older churches, or places of great natural beauty that facilitate a mystical awareness of God. One participant suggested, "A peaceful place, a place that takes you out of the hustle and bustle. That could be a spiritual or mystical place." A participant identified the priory church, where Hilton lived, as such a place. This participant stated, "And actually Thurgarton is rather like that. It's very lovely when you go down there, and it's very peaceful." Participants named prayer as a means of experiencing something mystical or bringing a greater awareness of God. One participant also wanted to add "social political commitment to justice" as a means of encountering the presence of God.

One group discussed the terms mystic and contemplative. This group was uncomfortable with individuals identifying themselves as mystics. One participant said, "It sounds a bit boastful if I'm honest. Some people have said things like that and immediately I have alarm bells." Another participant agreed, adding, "Hotlines to God can be very dangerous." The importance of a mystic or contemplative having accountability and experience with a wider community was mentioned. Julian of Norwich was given as an example, for while she was an anchoress in a cell, she was also attached to a church community and regularly engaged with individuals seeking spiritual guidance at her window. Speaking of Hilton, a participant said, "But in the community he would also experience a collective mysticism." Several participants also thought that many Christians have experienced moments of mystical encounter, such as prayer without words and more, but would not identify themselves as mystics. Thus, it might be important to use other terms (such as contemplative) or define the terms mystic and mysticism when working with individuals or groups. One participant offered the following definition of a mystic, which received much interest and affirmation from the group, "A mystic is someone who is open to the unknowability of God."

Second Movement: Hilton and The Three States of Christian Life

The second movement of the conversation shifted to the following question and concern, narrated similarly as,

> For Hilton, and the larger spiritual tradition of which he was a part, the goal of the Christian life was union with God. For centuries before Hilton, it was thought that the best way to pursue union with God was by becoming a contemplative, a monk or nun, and retreating from the world in order to devote oneself fully to prayer and contemplation. This contrasted with the majority of Christians, who were actives, with responsibilities in the world that prevented them from seriously seeking union with God. Hilton emphasized the possibility of a mixed life that is neither fully contemplative nor fully active, but a mixture. This mixed way opens the door for Christians living in the world to pursue union with God. What do you think about these three ways or states of life, starting with the contemplative, but also considering the active and mixed states, as he would have described them?

Both groups wrestled with making each of these states separate from the others. Several participants wanted to affirm the possibility that Christians participate in all three states at different times. One participant said, "Some people maintain that you can be contemplative and active at the same time." Another participant challenged the traditional idea that union with God was only, ordinarily, obtainable via the contemplative state, "Sorry. I would question the union with God, as being only available if you retreat from the world." Others affirmed this, which led to a discussion of Hilton's view that contemplation, of a significant kind, was available to lay people living in the world, especially if they adopt the mixed life. Individuals in both groups also connected the three traditional states as being possibilities for different life seasons. That is, they tied the active life to the raising of children and early career efforts and the contemplative life to life in retirement and advanced age. Yet, the possibility for moments of contemplation remained for those in active states, "It was sort of going through your day with everything being part of a prayer, which for a number of us who at the time, had young children, was a big impact on our lives."

Participants agreed that modern people are less comfortable with strong demarcations between the states of life. At the same time, after giving greater definition to the states of life, especially as Hilton and other medieval writers understood them, both groups recognized that the active life and mixed life are for most Christians. Prayer (the Jesus Prayer[6] was mentioned more than once), silence, and retreat were mentioned as ways for active and mixed life Christians to engage in moments of contemplation, which help to sustain their active lives. Both groups mentioned the possibility of an individual joining a religious order as a way of embracing the contemplative life. In one group, different participants added that someone could "be a solitary" or "join one of the enclosed communities." The group discussed how Hilton had tried the solitary approach of being a hermit before joining a community. Several participants affirmed the importance of being called to the contemplative life. A participant voiced this sentiment, "I think if you say I want to become a contemplative, there must be something stirring in you to actually move you down that road, working in you of the Holy Spirit."

Both groups raised the topic of whether clergy were called to the contemplative life. One group discussed this in greater detail. Clergy participants and non-clergy participants struggled with this idea. Participants saw the ceaseless activity that characterizes the life of many clergy as an obstacle to living a life of contemplation, especially in the traditional state as understood by Hilton and other writers. Traditionally, a life of contemplation meant withdrawal from the world. Almost by definition, clergy today are set apart and tasked to be active among people. The possibility of a mixed life for clergy, as Hilton and others envisioned, was seen as challenging

---

6. Mattewes-Green, *The Jesus Prayer*.

to realize in practice. Both groups discussed the need for the Church to create more space for silence and contemplation. Otherwise, according to participants, those with contemplative leanings will not come into faith communities or will not find an answer to their internal yearnings for contemplation within the Christian faith. One participant added, "I just wonder if Christianity hasn't got too little contemplation to draw people."

Third Movement: Hilton and the Means of Contemplation

The third movement of the interviews was framed using a question similar to,

> Hilton, and the spiritual tradition of his time, saw the principal work of Christians in the active way as that of charity, understood as love of neighbor. The principal work of contemplatives was different and focused on specifically seeking union with God. He recommends three means or practices of contemplation: (1) The reading of Holy Scripture, (2) meditation, and (3) diligent prayer with devotion. How do you imagine these three practices might help people to achieve union with God?

One group explored the concept of Scriptural reading as meditating, thinking carefully and imaginatively over a text, versus more contemporary understandings of meditation as a clearing of the mind. One participant shared how her own experience of developing a regular practice of reading Scripture was helpful to her, "It was so relevant to some of the stuff that I'm going through or have been going through." The participant added, referring to Scripture reading and study, that "very much about it helped me to become more contemplative." This same group had an extended conversation about the role of Scripture in different Anglican traditions. One participant shared, "the practice within a low evangelical church is to read scripture . . . spend half an hour having a quiet time . . . was something that was a real habit and part of your Christian journey." The same participant shared that through this practice, "God was revealing to you" and then you were "Listening and waiting on God."

In terms of prayer, both groups discussed the importance of praying with others. A participant shared, "Some people can find it easy to do on their own. I find it better in a group because I'm not disciplined enough to do it on my own." One group contrasted prayer with devotion, as prayer was "just mechanical." Another participant added that prayer with devotion would be "Not doing it because you're meant to." That is, not simply praying because it is an obligation. The Jesus Prayer was mentioned again as a type of prayer that is "actually practicing standing in Jesus' presence." This is the purpose and focus of contemplative practice.

One group further explored the importance of community in pursuing a contemplative life by asking, "Whether these three dimensions of contemplation should be individual as well as collective." This brought back the previously discussed idea of "collective mysticism." At first, different religious orders were given as examples of communities of collective contemplation. However, the group then discussed how these practices are present, at least in part, when Christians gather, in "Bible study" and "liturgy." As one participant said, "It's happening in every structure." The fact that these three means of contemplation are offered in many Christian gatherings, especially liturgical ones,[7] was recognized as being true, while also recognized as not being something the average worshiper is intentionally engaging. The question of the Eucharist as a means of contemplation was raised. It was discussed that the Eucharist was not a focus of Hilton's writings, though he makes passing reference to it and the sacrament of the Penance. Lastly, a participant suggested, "I could experience God through nature." Earlier, both groups discussed this as a possibility.

Fourth Movement: Hilton and Moderation in the Spiritual Life

The fourth movement of the interviews was framed using the following question,

> "Walter Hilton wrote, 'For with regard to your bodily nature, it is good to use discretion in eating, drinking, and sleeping, and in every kind of bodily penance: either in prolonged vocal prayer or in bodily feeling from great fervor of devotion—as in weeping or the like and in spiritual imagining as well, when one feels no grace. In all these kinds of work it is good to keep discretion, perhaps by breaking off sometimes; for moderation is best.'[8] What does this mean to you? How does it relate to the practice of your faith and spirituality?"

Both groups identified the word moderation and affirmed it as wise counsel. One group moved from moderation in eating to gratitude in eating,

---

7. Fagerberg, *Liturgical Mysticism*.
8. Clark and Dorward, *Walter Hilton: The Scale of Perfection*, 96.

"When you were eating, you think about what it is you're eating, maybe where it was grown, the people who picked it, harvested it, transported it, and then got into shops." The other group moved into a consideration of the fruits of the Holy Spirit, "Moderation is one of the fruits of the Holy Spirit, isn't it?" The discussion connected self-control with moderation.[9] One participant said, "I think we have a word for it today, which is holistic and balance." This same group made connections with moderation and Hilton's counsel to the idea of discretion, "He's also thinking of discretion in the other direction, that you don't want to overdo certain kinds of ascetic practices." In reply to this comment, another participant added, "Don't torture yourself in other words." Mindfulness was also seen as related to or made possible by moderation, "It's almost like mindfulness about everything that you do and then as part of that being aware, not concentrating on yourself all the time, but being aware of when something may need adjusting or confessing or something like that." A participant in the other group brought up the idea of moderation as being a particularly English trait. The group resonated with this, "One of them was moderation in all things, things we say about ourselves. Moderation in all things. And I suppose that's how Anglicans would view ourselves, isn't it? Moderate in all things."

Fifth Movement: Conclusion

The fifth and final movement of the interviews involved the following questions, "How might Walter Hilton and his teachings be a resource or help to the spiritual life today? What might be some helpful ways to connect people with Hilton and his teachings?" Both groups felt they did not know enough about Hilton to answer this question as fully as they would have liked. They acknowledged that knowledge of Hilton was scarce, even in the lands of Hilton, "Now if you were to ask most English people, including people who live around here, they would not know who he was." One participant shared, "I was hoping that one of the things when we met now, is to hear from you." However, each group also had responses to how Hilton could be a resource for Christians in their own vicinity and more widely. They pointed to Hilton's teaching as encouraging a "rhythm of life" leading to a "rich life." A participant stated, "If you want to enjoy the richness of life, you need moderation." One group asked the author to contribute

---

9. Gal 5:22–23: "By contrast, the fruit of the Spirit is love, joy, peace, patience, kindness, generosity, faithfulness, gentleness, and self-control."

ways in which Hilton might be a resource. The author offered several suggestions. All of which were affirmed by the group, but especially Hilton's view that laypeople could develop a serious spirituality, the concept of the spiritual life being akin to a fire requiring kindling, and how Hilton's writings provide, in a short space, a good entry into the spiritual theology of the centuries leading up to his time. There was some discussion about the changing social climate in Britain and the sense of unease that some are experiencing. One participant shared that Hilton might be a resource, "Britain as a country is searching for something."

The continued interest in alternative, non-Christian, and sometimes new-age spiritualities was discussed. The group thought Hilton might capture the interest of this group currently seeking spirituality outside of the Church. The group also thought Hilton would be a resource for those within the Church seeking a deeper spirituality. Another participant echoed this sense by saying, "It seems as though he's trying to draw Christians into a state of being . . . that would be useful today, because, for a lot of Christians, Christianity is a state of doing." One group spent some time discussing the need for local observances and resources: a brochure to give pilgrims to Thurgarton and Southwell, a Hilton day, and an icon[10] of Hilton (there is no current icon of him to anyone's knowledge). The participants discussed the need for a popular and more general commentary on Hilton's works. Several of the participants said his writings were difficult to understand, even in the contemporary translations. For example, one participant said, "It's quite difficult to read his own writings because it has its own kind of style of writing that has its own rhythm." Others suggested that podcasts or audio readings of books might be another way for people to engage with Hilton's writings and teachings. Walking is a popular pastime in the region, and it was suggested, "The Hilton walk be added to our local long walks." A walking pilgrimage from the Minster in Southwell to Thurgarton has been happening for the last couple of years. The thought is to have this route put into an official map and leaflet and distribute it widely. This has now been accomplished and the map is available online.

---

10. A religious depiction of Jesus, Mary, or a saint used for meditative and contemplative purposes. As an aide to worship and encounter with God. See Jim Forest, *Praying with Icons*.

REFLECTION ON RESEARCH APPROACH

The group discussions were fruitful. They indicate the potential for further empirical research within practical spiritual theology. At least two additional discussion groups would have made for a fuller research sample and experience. Also, participants in both groups shared their wish to know more about Walter Hilton. More familiarity with Hilton among the participants could have made these discussions richer. This could have been done informally by asking the participants to have read a preparatory paper about Hilton, read the *Mixed Life* and discussed it informally, or by having the researcher do a presentation about Hilton before each of the semi-structured group interviews. While this would likely result in greater engagement with Hilton and his ideas, it might have discouraged participants from sharing more of their own experiences. Also, gaining permission to use the many informal conversations the researcher had with individuals and groups about Walter Hilton and the spiritual life during the last research trip, if not previous trips, would have provided a wealth of insight and data.

In future research, using Thomas Groome's five-movement model of Shared Christian Praxis[11] is envisioned. This approach would address some of the weaknesses outlined above and the desire of all participants to know more about Walter Hilton—or the mystic being researched—before engaging in the semi-structured interviews. The focusing activity could involve a very brief introduction to Walter Hilton as a man of prayer. The first movement could invite participants to name and reflect on their own practice of prayer. The second movement could invite participants to reflect more critically on their lives of prayer by challenging them to define prayer, the reasons why they pray, and what they hope prayer will accomplish. The third movement could present Walter Hilton as a teacher of prayer and the spiritual life. Further biographical information would be given, but the heart of this movement would be presenting a select number of his teachings on the spiritual life. The fourth movement would encourage participants to reflect on their own experience of prayer and the spiritual life in light of Hilton and his teachings. The fifth movement could lead to a series of intentions, new awareness, or steps the participants intend to take in

---

11. Groome's Model: Focusing activity. Movements: 1) Naming/Expressing Present Praxis. 2) Critical Reflection on Present Action 3) Making Accessible Christian Story and Vision 4) Dialectical Hermeneutic to Appropriate Christian Story/Vision to Participants' Stories and Visions 5) Decision/Response for Living Christian Faith. See Groome, 146–48.

their lives of prayer. Also, this movement could identify ideas that might develop into new spiritual theologies, born out of the dialectical wisdom between Hilton and the participants. While not possible or advisable in every research project, a longer project could extend these sessions over a long period of time, following participants' efforts at implementing new intentions and in developing the details of new practical spiritual theologies.

TENTATIVE PRACTICAL SPIRITUAL THEOLOGIES

Participants shared many valuable insights into the spiritual life. In addition, their responses to Hilton were illuminative, especially regarding aspects of his teaching that might be helpful to others. Several ideas the group discussed could be further developed into theological practices, reflections, and guidance that could resource the spiritual lives of Christians today. Three will be explored here that bears particular attention and could form the basis of further writing and research. These ideas are tentative and not fully developed. Further development of each would constitute an exercise in practical spiritual theology.

Collective Mysticism

The idea that Hilton would have experienced a collective mysticism by living in a community at the Augustinian priory in Thurgarton was mentioned more than once. Many mystics over the centuries lived in a religious community. This is not always clear from reading their writings. For example, in most of Hilton's works, he is writing to individuals. The group thought of Hilton's sharing in the common life of prayer and worship in the Augustinian community in Thurgarton as providing an atmosphere conducive to the experience of God. A practical spiritual theology of collective mysticism could be developed providing guidelines for those seeking to develop their life of prayer and their life with God. Much of Hilton's counsel, even to solitaries, points to the necessity of community, specifically the Church. Hilton's counsels could be reflected on and adapted for contemporary Christians, with specific groups empirically researched. For example, two sets of research groups could investigate participants' experience in implementing Hilton's counsel on personal prayer and contemplation. One set of research participants would pursue Hilton's counsel on their own, with only occasional check-ins from the researcher. The other set of research participants would pursue Hilton's counsel within a small group. The experiences of the groups and the individuals could be explored through semi-structured interviews and other means. The similarities and differences in participants' experiences might prove useful in understanding how individuals pray and how individuals grow in the practice of regular prayer.

A collective mysticism, a collective posture of openness toward union with God, finds Biblical support in St. Paul's famous analogy of the Body of Christ.[12] It suggests that as much as a mystic's encounter with God may seem to be an individual and private experience, it actually contributes to the well-being of the entire Body of Christ. A spiritual theology of collective mysticism strengthens the suggestions made in the last chapter for there being a mystic dimension to Christian Education, as well as the concept of conative mysticism. This collective approach means that cultivating mysticism, an openness to the experience of God, is a vocation for all Christians. According to author and spiritual director Evelyn Underhill, "We cannot say that there is a separate 'mystical sense,' which some men have and some not, but rather that every human soul has a certain latent capacity for God, and that in some this capacity is realized with an astonishing richness."[13] A vocation and a call to experience God according to each individual's gifts, calling, and situation. The love of God draws the entire body of Christ toward deeper intimacy and communion with the Trinity. One group shared their belief that many Christians have mystical or numinous experiences, but do not have the language to talk about them. A commitment to collective mysticism means a commitment to a mystic dimension to all spiritual formation. Spiritual formation that equips worshippers, spiritual directees, and students not only to recognize their experiences of God but a spiritual formation that gives them language to speak about these intelligibly and comfortably.

There is a mysterious pneumatological reality to this collective mysticism that unites all Christians together across time and space. This is the work of the Holy Spirit. A collective mysticism is a facet of the ancient Christian doctrine of the communion of saints.[14] This is the mystery of the reality, that the anchoress hidden away from the world, is blessing the entire Body of Christ through her prayer and her drawing near to God. The outpouring of God's love she receives draws the entire Body a little

---

12. 1 Cor 12:12–27.
13. Underhill, *The Mystics of the Church*, 4.
14. Walford, *Communion of Saints*.

closer to Christ. There is also the visible, corporate reality of Christians being gathered together at a particular time and place. This is the life of local congregations and religious communities, with all their human encouragements and challenges. This is the embodied, incarnate, work of the Spirit in a small congregation gathering together on a Sunday or when one Christian visits another and they share a prayer over a cup of coffee. An affirmation of both realities, the unseen work of the Spirit and the visible work of the Body, characterizes a theology of collective mysticism.[15] The spiritual life, even for the solitary, is never a life alone.

From States of Life to Stages of Life

Both groups wondered about the medieval concept of a state of life as being lifelong. They did not deny that some are clearly called to the active life, the mixed life, and the contemplative life, but they wondered if these states of life might also be conceived of as stages of life. An exploration of each state of life and how it might relate to human seasons of life could develop a practical spiritual theology of life development from ascetical and mystical theological perspectives.[16] This approach could be liberating and sustaining for individual Christians and Christian communities.

For example, many of the participants thought of the contemplative life as being a potentially enriching and life-changing focus for adults in the third season of life. Not that all older adults would become full-fledged contemplatives, but that many would find a sense of usefulness, challenge, and comfort in pursuing a serious life of prayer. Likewise, those in the first season of life could find help and structure in the traditional emphasis of the active life. For example, the young mother should not feel guilty for not spending an hour in silent prayer every day but could intentionally embrace her present season of life, as aligning with the active state, where the chief work is of loving God and neighbor. Her prayer life may be cultivated through periods of short prayer and reflection throughout the day. A successful middle-aged professional feeling a desire to live a more intentionally spiritual life does not have to leave everything and go to the monastery. She could, as Hilton recommended centuries ago, embrace the mixed life.

---

15. Andrews, *The Kingdom Life*. See Chapter Two: "Communities of Grace" and Chapter Nine: "The Holy Spirit and Spiritual Formation."
16. Balswick, *The Reciprocating Self*.

Contemplative Evangelization

One participant wondered whether present-day churches were quiet enough to draw people who might be inclined to reflection and contemplation. One group also mentioned the importance of churches making time for silence in their worship services. A practical spiritual theology of contemplative evangelism could be developed by engaging in research and reflection about where people seek out silence already and how the church can participate in, mirror, or offer similar opportunities. Many community centers offer classes on yoga, mindfulness, and secular forms of meditation. These are often well attended. They point to a hunger experienced by many people for spiritual practice and experience. As one of the groups discussed, many of these individuals are drawn to these alternative spiritualities. This should not be surprising if we take Hilton and other mystics' counsel seriously that human beings were created to seek union with God. Contemplative evangelistic efforts could experiment with offering classes on the spiritual life to the public in approachable and non-threatening ways.

The use of silence in worship could also be explored. Specifically, how individuals encounter and respond to silence in worship. Formal research could be done with silent prayer groups as well as those who have never practiced any form of silent prayer, but who, throughout the course of the study, begin to do so. The idea of evangelizing culture by providing space for reflection, silence, and stillness has implications for church architecture, art, music, worship, schedules, and more.[17] Churches that open their doors to provide a quiet place for personal reflection are already participating in what might be called contemplative evangelization. Silence is widely acknowledged as an important part of traditional Christian practice.[18] Author and priest Henri Nouwen writes, "The Desert Fathers praise silence as the safest way to God."[19] Monasteries and other sacred places are often characterized by their silence. If silence is a doorway that can invite human reflection on life. A reflection that sometimes turns toward God, then Christians have a responsibility and a missional mandate to provide opportunities for silence. Alongside providing opportunities for silence, Christians should instruct themselves and others on how to cultivate silence in

---

17. Some contemplative considerations for evangelism are explored in the following work: Heath, *The Mystic Way of Evangelism*.

18. Nouwen, *The Way of the Heart*; Barton, *Invitation to Solitude and Silence*.

19. Nouwen, *The Way of the Heart*, 25.

everyday life. To give guidance on how silence can be conducive to prayer, to self-knowledge, and a way of opening the self to the experience of God.

Moderation as an English Virtue

Both groups were drawn to Hilton's teaching on moderation. One participant verbalized moderation as being a particularly English virtue. This idea resonated strongly with the group. Both groups were drawn to the discussion of moderation. Moderation or any virtue would benefit from a general theological reflection. What are the popular, cultural understandings of moderation? What do Scripture and the history of the Christian tradition have to say about moderation? Are there subtle or glaring gaps between these various sources? Research with English participants might focus on why moderation resonates with so many as an English virtue. This would require cultural exploration and evaluation. The group might be invited to consider if their English sense of moderation is challenged at all by their Christian commitments. If the English sense of moderation is seen as a positive, even for Christians, how might that virtue be incorporated into ordinary Christian life? This would result in a spiritual theology of moderation that is localized to English contexts. A similar research procedure with Americans might result in a different understanding of moderation. This example highlights the wisdom of practical theology's focus on theologizing for specific settings and avoiding universalizing theories. A comparison of moderation research projects would yield greater insight into the virtue and practice of moderation from a Christian perspective.

CONTEMPORARY CHRISTIANS AND PRACTICAL SPIRITUAL THEOLOGY

Practical spiritual theology as a theological method is done for the benefit of contemporary Christians. Its purpose is to retrieve the wisdom of past mystics for the faith and practice of Christians today. While analysis of theological and sociological writings is a valuable part of this process of retrieval, the presentation of a mystic to actual Christians is essential to the method. This commitment reflects an affirmation of the wisdom of ordinary believers. The Church has sometimes called this the *sensus fidelium*, the sense of the faithful.[20] Theology is done by professional theologians, as well as practitioners such as lay and ordained ministers, spiritual directors, and educators. However, every Christian in their own way is a participant in the work of theology. The Church has not always affirmed the positive role of the laity in shaping theological concerns and practices, even on topics that profoundly affect their lives.

Practical spiritual theology affirms a positive sense of what is sometimes called ordinary theology. Jeff Astley writes, "It is my belief that the study of ordinary theology... should recover theology as a fundamental dimension of piety, an inherent part of every Christian's vocation." He defines ordinary theology in part as his concern to "take seriously the beliefs of 'non-theologically educated' churchgoers and other Christian believers."[21] Drawing upon all the theological resources for the sake of contemporary faith and practice is the commitment of practical spiritual theology. This means drawing upon the scholarly acumen of theologians in the academy, practitioners in the Church, and laity who live out their faith, for the most part, in wider society.

---

20. Whitehead and Whitehead, *Method in Ministry*, 10–11.
21. Astley, *Ordinary Theology*, viii.

Chapter 5

Possibilities of Practical Spiritual Theology

AN EMERGING APPROACH TO CONTEMPORARY SPIRITUAL THEOLOGY

Christianity claims that the present is persuasive. The faith that was lived yesterday, must be lived today. The context and content of the past are different from the present. This necessitates a faith that has continuity with the past as well as an orientation toward the future. Navigating the present moment faithfully requires wisdom about the ways of God and the ways that lead to God. Practical spiritual theology seeks to retrieve the wisdom of mystics, like Walter Hilton, to resource and inspire the spiritual lives of Christians today. It is one way, among many, of studying the Christian mystics. It is a method that is explicitly theological and pastoral. It results in new and renewed formulations of spiritual theology for the Church's present faith and practice. It is a method that encourages partnerships between scholars and practitioners in the fields of ministry, spiritual direction, and education. It embraces theological insights from professional theologians, ministry practitioners, and the laity.

For centuries, mystical writers have guided individuals seeking an encounter and experience with God. Their wisdom is derived from Scripture, the Church's teaching, as well as their own experience of the spiritual life and the experience of those they guided. Seekers of spirituality and faith, as well as church leaders, have often given these mystics a special authority. An authority born of holiness. An authority rooted in the mystics' experience of the divine and guiding others toward the divine. Mystics are witnesses, like bonfires on a dark winter's night, to the reality of God. Walter Hilton, a fourteenth-century, English mystic, proved to be an excellent first case study for the development of practical spiritual theology. His major writings are accessible in good English translations.[1] He is often referred to in discussions of medieval English spirituality but is not as well-known as is his near contemporary, Julian of Norwich. His writings are systematic, covering a wide range of topics related to the spiritual life. He innovated by opening the door for serious spirituality not only for contemplatives, but for laypeople in the world with active responsibilities.[2]

Practical spiritual theology combines the wisdom of past spiritual theology with the tools and insights of practical theology. Spiritual theology, especially in the forms written by Hilton and others, is inherently concerned with a way of life. A way of life in accord with the truths of theology and the content of revelation. It is a work of spiritual formation. Hilton wrote to individuals whose interest in spiritual matters was not theoretical, nor casual, but personal and vocational. The anchoress he writes to in *The Scale* is actively seeking union with God. The secular lord he writes to in *The Mixed Life* is wrestling with whether he should lay aside his secular responsibilities to embrace the contemplative life. Hilton's guidance was directed to specific individuals and their situations. Likewise, practical spiritual theology does not create universal theologies for all times and places, but practices and theologies tailored to specific times and places.

Thomas Groome's model of Shared Christian Praxis proved to be unusually suited for the tasks of practical spiritual theology. Originally, Groome was intended only to be a conversation partner with Hilton. Further reflection determined that Groome offered critical components toward the method and methodology of practical spiritual theology. Groome's model encourages participants to move from a consideration of their life experience to the story of the Christian faith, and then back to their life experience. The goal of this exercise is lived Christian faith. This helpfully situates the wisdom of the past with an orientation toward the present. The work of retrieval is foundational to practical spiritual theology. This work is helped by Groome's emphasis on the Christian story.

Narrative and story are central to the human experience and the Christian tradition. Many of the saints and mystics are known to us by stories. Mystics and saints not only offer concrete teachings and spiritual practices

1. Clark and Dorward, *Walter Hilton: The Scale of Perfection*.
2. McGinn, *Varieties of Vernacular Mysticism*, 373.

Possibilities of Practical Spiritual Theology

that can be adapted by contemporary believers for their own spiritual lives, but they inspire and motivate others to live the faith in their own times and places. The motivational value of the witness of the saints, attested to over the centuries,[3] is a powerful resource for the lives of Christians today. The challenge of Christian discipleship, of following Jesus, takes on flesh and blood in many times, places, and life situations through the witness of other imperfect human beings. This gives contemporary Christians hope that as the saints and mystics sought God faithfully in their own times so they may do so today.

An Overview of the Method

The method of practical spiritual theology is flexible. There is more than one way to retrieve the wisdom of a medieval mystic in order to resource the faith and practice of Christians today. As has been explored throughout this book, the method has four major movements: I) Select a Mystic, II) Research a Mystic, III) Suggest New or Renewed Practice, and IV) Live and Share the Practice. The second movement consists of four steps. First, research and reflection on a mystic. This is the research on the mystic's life. Their history, ideas, and how others have interacted with their ideas. Second, research and reflection on a contemporary thinker. This is the research on one or more thinkers whose ideas will be brought into dialogue with the mystic's ideas. Third, conversation with contemporary Christians. This may involve formal empirical research or informal presentation and discussion. Fourth, theological reflection toward practice. This is where a creative synthesis between old and new ideas may take place. It is also where an old practice, concept, or understanding may be reformulated for the present. Like other methods and models of theological reflection, the movements and steps can be envisioned sequentially as well as cyclically. This method may be adapted for formal and informal research purposes according to the needs of the researcher or researching community.

The entry point into the method may be driven by a curiosity about a particular mystic or driven by a specific research question. For example, an

---

3. This is attested to by the fact that Roman Catholic, Eastern Orthodox, Anglican, and most mainline Protestant denominations all follow a liturgical calendar full of observances of saints and Christians from the past. Supporting these observances are books with prayers, biographies, and stories about the saints. For example, see Episcopal Church, *Lesser Feasts and Fasts*. See also Thurston and Attwater, *Butler's Lives of the Saints*. See also Knox, *Foxe's Book of Martyrs*.

individual or group may select Julian of Norwich as a subject for practical spiritual theological research simply because they are curious about her. They may have an intuition that her writings can inspire their faith and practice today. Alternatively, her writings may have already inspired the researcher to study her more formally. Conversely, during the pandemic, many studied Julian because of her experience with living in a voluntary enclosure. They studied her hoping to find inspiration from her life of faith in the past for their own in the present.[4] There is not always consensus about who counts as a mystic. Researchers and research groups can use the material in this book in determining their definitions. It is recommended to select mystics who have extant writings. It may be possible to use this method using the collected stories and traditions about a particular mystic. This approach must acknowledge the distance between many accounts of mystics' lives and the words and lives of the mystics themselves. Such a project presents some interpretive and hermeneutical challenges.

All research with this method asks how a mystic can inspire the faith and practice of Christians today. However, some researchers may have more specific research questions that fall under this general inquiry. For example, a group may study Catherine of Siena to discover how her life of prayer and social witness can resource and inspire the social justice efforts of their campus ministry. A group of spiritual directors may study the letters of Catherine of Siena to discover how her approach to spiritual guidance might resource and inspire their own practice of spiritual direction. A theologian may research Richard Rolle's theology of mystical song and warmth in conversation with a contemporary Pentecostal theologian to discover if Rolle might be a bridge between medieval mystical forms of spirituality and modern charismatic forms of spirituality. Like with any research question, the nature of the question and the line of its inquiry may change or develop over the time of the research project.

This method, reflecting its synthesis of practical theology and spiritual theology, is oriented toward lived Christian faith. Therefore, the final step, of the four research movements, is theological reflection toward practice. The final step involves not only articulating new or retrieved practice but living it. This theological reflection leading to lived practice is oriented toward, at least, the Christians who participated in the study. The study may have implications and insights for Christians in a variety of contexts, but it must first be oriented toward the group or community that participated

---

4. Fox, *Julian of Norwich*.

in the research. The possibilities for practice that arise out of research will vary. In some cases, a practice may be retrieved. For example, a congregation researching Walter Hilton may introduce the practice of spiritual direction to their church. While the practice of Christian spiritual direction is ancient, it was not known or valued by the congregation until completing their research on Hilton. In other cases, a practice may be reformulated, as the research in Southwell suggested for the medieval concept of the state of life.

It is not necessary to conduct research about mystics in the places they lived. However, this can be a fruitful project, as research in Southwell demonstrated. Studying mystics in a variety of communities will yield greater insights and a variety of new and reformulated practices that are embodiments of traditional and renewed spiritual theologies. This will strengthen the Church's faith and witness around the world. This method affirms the value of mystics for many Christians, across denominations, traditions, cultures, and social locations. When conducting formal academic research there are protocols required of the researcher by their academic institution.[5] Protocols that are intended to protect human beings from harm, whether intentional or accidental. Without following these procedures, such research cannot be published in scholarly publications. Formal research also requires a level of advanced academic training. This means that most formal practical spiritual theological research will probably be conducted by scholars, as well as graduate students or ministry practitioners pursuing or holding advanced degrees.[6]

Scholars will not always be residents in the communities where they conduct their research. Researchers should strive to get to know the community and be among them as fellow pilgrims on the path of the spiritual life, not just as a professional theologians dropping by. This attention to a particular setting and people is an essential commitment of practical theology. The author was blessed to share worship, tea, and laughter, as well as time in conversation with a variety of people in Southwell during visits there over the years. An advantage of informal research using this method is that the facilitation of the project can sometimes be done locally. This is an advantage in helping a group or community persist in living the results of the research. Even with informal research projects, there are advantages

---

5. Creswell, *Research* Design, 95.

6. A practical spiritual theological approach could be utilized by Doctor of Ministry students in completing their final thesis or project.

to bringing in a scholar or someone familiar with the method to facilitate the process.

Some suggestions are included in the appendixes for informal use of the practical spiritual theological method by students, groups, and faith communities. The flexibility of the practical spiritual theological method is intended to make it useful for formal and informal research in a variety of settings. The method envisions small groups and faith communities becoming mystical laboratories, researchers of the Spirit, conducting their own investigations into the mystics to inspire and resource their faith and practice. These local experiments in practical spiritual theology can then be shared with other scholars, practitioners, and faith communities. Theologian David Tracey argued that theology is responsible to and should address itself to three publics—Church, Society, and Academy.[7] The possibilities of the project of practical spiritual theology will now be considered from the perspective of each of these publics.

PRACTICAL SPIRITUAL THEOLOGY AND THE THREE PUBLICS

Church

Practical spiritual theology is inherently ecclesial. Mystics, like Hilton, wrote from within the Church to others within the Church. The beliefs and practices they commend assume a Christian perspective and commitment. The work of retrieval will be important in helping contemporary Christians wrestle with their perspectives and commitments and how these are shaped by their Christian faith as well as other influences. The development of the concept of conative mysticism may also help some in the Church see new possibilities with mystics that they may have been previously dismissed as "so heavenly minded they are of no earthly good." The Western Church's history is rich with mystical and spiritual writers. Individuals or teams of researchers could spend their lives developing new spiritual theologies based on dialectical engagement with past mystics and contemporary Christians. A focus on one mystic or a group of mystics could also be the focus of a scholar's career. Likewise, faith communities or practitioners of spiritual formation could engage fruitfully with a mystic or group of mystics for many years. For some mystics, there is translation work to be done.

---

7. Tracy, *The Analogical Imagination*, 3–46.

Possibilities of Practical Spiritual Theology

For many, there is the need for historical and theological reflection on their writings. Besides this, even mystics with a small corpus of writings could engage a scholar for a large part of their career if they engaged in extensive empirical research with groups of people over longer periods of time.

It will be helpful if some researchers and faith communities engage the historic locales or cultures of given mystics. As with Walter Hilton and the Southwell region in England, this kind of engagement may help to revitalize or at least bring renewed attention to certain aspects of Christian spirituality, discipleship, and life associated with a particular region or place. Over the course of the author's years of traveling to and being in correspondence with individuals in Southwell, the awareness of Hilton has increased. Along with a sense that more should be done to promote awareness of his life and teachings. Hilton's church in Thurgarton is now listed on the site of the British Pilgrimage Trust.[8] At least three walking pilgrimages from Southwell to Thurgarton have taken place during this time.

There is still much to be done in promoting Hilton within the lands of Hilton, which illustrates that the fruits of practical spiritual theology will take time. Christians in local contexts will need to be inspired and equipped to carry on the long haul of efforts to promote local mystics. Part of that inspiration and equipping may be the writing or creating of resources on practical spiritual theology that are accessible to laity and clergy alike. The need for these kinds of resources on Walter Hilton was raised in the research groups during the author's trips to the Southwell region. Churches with ties to historic mystics, saints, and other figures have a responsibility to steward the witness of these disciples from the past. This is especially true of churches named after a mystic, and those with a historical connection to a mystic. In these situations and others, it is possible to conceive of extended, long-term practical spiritual theological initiatives and projects. Spreading awareness about and encouraging engagement with Walter Hilton in the Southwell region and beyond is one example of such a long-term initiative.

Besides prioritizing the fire of their faith, a powerful next step for practitioners (including for scholars when they teach) is to prioritize spiritual formation in all aspects of their work. Traditions and denominations use different terms and sometimes use the same terms differently to describe the work of spiritual formation. Whatever term is used, be it Christian education, religious education, discipleship, or something else, these

---

8. The British Pilgrimage Trust, "Southwell Minster Pilgrimage in a Day."

practitioners should reorient all their work toward lived Christian faith. Each practitioner according to their influence and responsibility should encourage this fundamental orientation toward spiritual formation in all aspects of the ministry, community, or organization they are a part of. This formational emphasis should be for all ages. While programming may be helpful, it should not be limited to programs. Transformative programs without integration into the rest of the ministry or organization tend to have limited impact. They often remain a side interest for a few instead of the first fruits of a new way of being together for all. The goal is to cultivate and nurture a culture of spiritual formation that is an ordinary and all-inclusive part of a given congregation or group's life together.

In increasingly secular societies, everyday Christians will need more, not less formation, to maintain everyday faith. It is impossible to make more than preliminary suggestions for how to do this for so many varied settings. A first step is to discern how to implement a mystic dimension into existing formation offerings, whether they are small groups, Bible studies, or sermons. Practitioners should begin with what is explicitly thought of as formational or educational in their setting. This is the place for formation leaders to begin to make changes, large or small, as they carefully and prayerfully discern them. Then over time, the leadership of a ministry, church, or institution can bring the mystic dimension to other areas of the organization's life. A practical spiritual theological investigation may be undertaken to discern how to do that. For example, an institution or congregation may study the writings of sixteenth-century Spanish mystic Teresa of Ávila, specifically her book, *The Interior Castle*,[9] to discern how to understand and utilize their buildings in new ways, integrating the physical stewardship of their buildings with the call to be stewards of the Spirit for the people they serve.

Starting with existing formational opportunities can be done in conjunction with or following a more general assessment of the spiritual vitality of a congregation, group, or community. This can be done informally. There are also several assessment tools available from different denominations and research groups that can clarify the inner life of a congregation or institution. Some questions that can begin to help a group prayerfully and carefully reflect on their spiritual vitality are these: "How dry is the spiritual kindling of your group, ministry, or congregation?" "Is it burning bright with the fire of God's love?" "Do you find yourselves in the company

---

9. Teresa of Ávila *The Interior Castle*.

of the mystics, being like bonfires on a cold winter's night, filling the world with warmth and light?" "What is at the heart of your life together?" "What warms up our community spiritually?" Spiritual directors and pastors can modify these questions or attend to them in various ways in their work of spiritual guidance. The conversations following these questions will suggest further questions, areas of investigation, as well as existing strengths to build upon. There are many tools and approaches for studying communities, from a variety of perspectives, that can be part of the work of understanding your setting.[10] Understanding your context is a vital part of all practical theological methods. Something else scholars and practitioners can do to help themselves and those they serve is to conduct their own research and reading on the mystics. It is not necessary to utilize a practical spiritual theological method when doing so. However, some suggestions for doing so are provided in the appendix. Prayerful reading and research can be "sticks" or "kindling" as Walter Hilton taught, igniting the fire of an individual's faith. Those engaged in the work of spiritual formation should give ongoing attention to tending the fire of their own faith. After their own faith, they should give priority to supporting the faith of their immediate family or friendship group. After this, they should prioritize the faith development of the key leaders and workers in their ministry, organization, or group.

Society

Christians live as a people within various societies. The Church must speak to these wider societies. Today, societies include those who are not Christian, those of other religious traditions, and the growing population of the unaffiliated in the Western world. How Christians in the West might faithfully respond to the trends of secularization and the Church's institutional decline vary. No more than a brief consideration of these responses can be considered here. One option that has gained significant attention, positive and constructive, in recent years is the so-called "Benedict Option."[11] The Benedict option, is named after the fifth and sixth-century founder of the Benedictine Order, Saint Benedict. The Benedict option suggests that in response to secularization, Christians should, at least in part, retreat from

---

10. Ammerman et al., *Studying Congregations*. See also Rendle and Mann, *Holy Conversations*. See also Moules et al., *Conducting Hermeneutic Research*.

11. Dreher, *The Benedict Option*.

the world into their own communities. In other words, to preserve a warm, vital, spiritual center. A flame to be cultivated, nurtured, and protected. This is to preserve a distinctively Christian culture of formation, discipleship, worship, and witness. There is another option, a Dominic Option[12] or to put it in Hiltonian terms: a Mixed Option.

Saint Dominic was the thirteenth-century founder of the Order of Preachers.[13] A Dominic option embraces both the necessity for warm centers of Christian living and the necessity for Christian engagement with the world. St. Dominic is traditionally pictured with a black and white dog with a flaming torch in its mouth. That torch is the fire of God. The fire of God, the mystical experience, must not be kept sequestered away in vital Christian communities, but cultivated, kindled, and carried out into the world as blazing spiritual torches by every Christian into every part of society. Before founding the Order of Preachers, St. Dominic was, like Hilton, an Augustinian Canon. This mixed option nurtures spiritualities and practices associated with all three states of life (i.e., active, mixed, contemplative). Contemplatives can dedicate their lives to tending the fire at the warm center of the community through prayer. Actives, probably the majority of Christians, can regularly break off from their responsibilities in the world by returning to the warm centers of their local faith communities, cultivating a warm center of faith in their own lives. Those pursuing the mixed life strive to live with a foot near the home fires and a foot out in the world. This Dominic option cultivates a mixed life model for Christian communities. The mixed life as taught by Hilton and others may be the ecclesiological and missiological posture needed by the Church in a secular age or as some have defined it, a post-secular age. This way of organizing the Church's life and work in the world mirrors, as Hilton and others have taught, Jesus' way of being in the world. Jesus' pattern of life flowed from private prayer, time with his disciples, and then time with his disciples engaging people and their needs in the wider world. If Jesus is the model for the Mixed Life, as Hilton teaches, Jesus can also be seen as the exemplar of conative

---

12. The Dominic option is the author's own counter vision to Dreher's which is essentially a mixed life option. Saint Dominic was an Augustinian Canon before he founded the Order of Preachers and the friars retained many elements of the religious life of canons. The idea of a Dominic option has since been discussed independently of the author in many settings, both prior to, and after the author's conception of such an option. Pecknold, "The Dominican Option."

13. Goergen, *St. Dominic: The Story of a Preaching Friar*. See also Woods, *Mysticism and Prophecy*.

mysticism. A mysticism that draws the mystic into intimacy with God and sends the mystic out into the world to love the things God loves.

A mixed option for Christian engagement in a secular world might further develop the idea from the Southwell interviews of conceiving the three classic states of life (active, contemplative, mixed) as seasons of life. This mixed option might also develop the ideas of collective mysticism and contemplative evangelization that also emerged from the research groups. Conative mysticism may prove an attraction to Nones and those whom Nancy Ammerman's research identifies as being extra-theistic. Despite the Church's decline in the West, interest in spirituality, meditation, creation, and self-improvement remains high. Places like Southwell and Thurgarton, which have historic, attractive, and beautiful churches, can combine their popularity as pilgrimage and tourist destinations with a promotion of local mystics and saints. This dual draw of historic buildings and historic personality may prove to be a powerful combination for creating channels of spiritual interest and practice that can flow in and out of congregations into their wider communities. The vitality and popularity of English Cathedrals, as exceptions to the story of the Church's decline in the United Kingdom, may have something to teach other churches, with and without historic buildings, about stewarding the witness of sacred places and persons.[14]

Work with individuals on and beyond the edges of the Church's life could be fruitful if approached from the perspective of practical spiritual theology. Careful presentation of a mystic to a variety of groups may yield fruitful insights as to which aspects of traditional Christian spirituality resonate with those who rarely, if ever, participate in the life of the Church. This serious engagement with the spiritual life of outsiders may prove an effective means of contemplative evangelism on its own. Some participants in the Southwell region thought that Hilton might have something to offer the wider British culture. A research project could be undertaken with the express purpose of engaging with people who do not attend any of the local churches in Southwell. Participants would be asked about their experience of spirituality, offering the experiences of Hilton, as a historical resident of the area, and as a conversation partner. The listening process to those outside of the boundaries of local churches could also be a means of contemplative evangelism, drawing those beyond the walls inside the walls. The presence of visible and historic buildings like Southwell Minster and the Priory Church in Thurgarton can help this work. However, engaging

---

14. Beeson, *The Deans*, 233. See also Shaw, "The Potential of Cathedrals."

the views of those outside the Church will increasingly require researchers to go outside of the boundaries of Christian buildings and spaces. This will be especially so in areas where the Church has no positive witness with the local community.

Bringing the wisdom of mystics and spiritual writers into dialogue with those beyond the Church may also help to contribute to a public theology of the spiritual life. Public theology is another subdiscipline of practical theology. Public theology is the study and practice of Christian engagement with wider society, especially non-Christian society.[15] Practical theology's ability to partner with other disciplines, such as sociology and psychology, may enable a public theology of the spiritual life to find a hearing among those who normally would not listen to the Church or individuals associated with the Christian faith. For example, questions of the nature of the spiritual life might be articulated for wider society as questions about what is a good life or what does it mean to be human? How can human beings flourish? What values and practices lead to human flourishing? These are all questions that Christians have reflected upon for centuries. Public theology asks how Christians can translate those questions and answers, those historical conversations about being human, to the wider society. In ways that outsiders to the faith can understand, using their terminologies and ways of speaking, as well as addressing their concerns.

This may sometimes require dropping Christian language, common and technical, in public theological conversations and finding ways to speak about the spiritual life that can be understood by many audiences within a given society. The interest in living a good life, a full life, and the interest in personal biography, especially of individuals who lived unusual lives is a cultural phenomenon. Certain mystics might prove attractive to those outside of the Church, giving them a vision of the Christian life they had not previously known or encountered.[16] Practical spiritual theology done for a wider public may enable and enrich conversations where ordinary spiritual theology, indeed, even ordinary Christian speech, is not welcome. Thomas Groome's focus on narrative and story could strengthen a public theology of the spiritual life.[17] Story continues to be a mode of communica-

---

15. For example, see Volf, *A Public Faith*. See also Williams, *Faith in the Public Square*.

16. The importance of the exemplar can be traced back to James, *Varieties of Religious Experience*, 43.

17. Individuals within and outside the church will likely engage with mystics and spiritual topics first based on actual experience and reflection, even on the level of limit-experience and limit language or on the level of Paul Tillich's conception of the ultimate

tion that resonates with most people across beliefs and situations. Experiments in public spiritual theology could be documentaries about mystics, plays about mystics, and works of creative fiction about mystics. In all cases, the forms of presentation need to be created with society as the intended principal audience, not the Church. Such projects will require extensive listening to and partnerships with those outside of the Church in order to be authentic.

Academy

The method and methodology of practical spiritual theology will benefit from additional resources that enable scholars and practitioners to retrieve the wisdom of the mystics for their own spiritual lives and the spiritual vitality of the communities they serve. This work will benefit from the rigor and intellectual resources of the academy. The use of empirical research methods, like semi-structured interview groups, is part of the toolbox of practical spiritual theology. This kind of research will benefit tremendously from the expertise of scholars trained in theological and sociological research methods. Not all practical spiritual theology will require university sponsored or affiliated research, but the overall project of practical spiritual theology will be greatly enriched by such research. Scholars from many social locations and faith postures are actively engaged in research and writing that will be of critical and affirmative value to the development of contemporary spiritual theologies. This is a theologically overt project and so practical spiritual theology research and work might best take place at an academic institution with a faith affiliation. The normative and directive elements of traditional spiritual theology are an essential part of practical spiritual theology and these might be difficult to articulate within institutions or by individuals without explicit Christian theological commitments.

The development of practical spiritual theologies from the perspective of various contextual and liberation theologies will be greatly enriched through the academy. Extensive work has been done in a variety of liberation theologies, theologies oriented toward the experiences of

---

concern, see Tillich, *The Essential Tillich*. Additionally, Tillich's claim on page 27 of the aforementioned title is useful for considerations of public theology and practical spiritual theology more generally: "For only in the community of spiritual beings is language alive. Without language there is no act of faith, no religious experience!" A narrative approach to methodology might, therefore, be most helpful in developing a public theology of the spiritual life.

and emancipatory ends for particular groups. Groups that have been and sometimes still are marginalized in all three publics. For example, there are Feminist theologies of all kinds,[18] Womanist and black theologies of all kinds[19], and Latinx theologies of all kinds to name a few.[20] A representative theologian from any of these theologies could be used as a conversation partner with a medieval mystic. This could result in a feminist spiritual theology of Julian of Norwich or a liberation theology of Catherine of Siena. Practical spiritual theology could be a way for theologians and communities to develop spiritualities that reflect their concerns while still being connected to the wider Christian tradition.[21]

Research could also be done with diverse groups, with representatives from many communities within a region or across them. This will result in the development of theologies and practices, that while not universal in their applicability, are nonetheless useful to the spiritual lives of Christians across a variety of sociological demographics. For example, a theology of shared prayer, ecumenical prayer, could be developed through an investigation into Brother Lawrence's classic, *Practicing the Presence of God*.[22] This could be a shared research project of say a Black Pentecostal congregation and a mostly white Episcopal congregation. A practical spiritual theological project like this might suggest ways in which formal liturgy and extemporaneous prayer, personal and public prayer, and reverence in worship and exaltation in worship, might resource and inspire the individual and shared work of social justice by both congregations in their community. While ecumenical and unitive projects are not always possible, the unitive possibilities of the practical spiritual theological method are desirable.

---

18. Ross, *Extravagant Affections*.

19. Copeland, *Enfleshing Freedom*.

20. Isasi-Diaz and Mendieta, *Decolonizing Epistemologies*.

21. A project that explores similar themes is Sobrino, *Spirituality of Liberation*. Sobrino writes on page 1 of this text, "Without the spiritual life, apostolic work would be threatened from within. It would be cut off from its deepest roots." Practical spiritual theology could be one way to help various liberation and contextual theologies to remain rooted in the roots of the Christian tradition avoiding the danger of theology shifting to become only excellent sociology.

22. Brother Lawrence of the Resurrection, *The Practice of the Presence of God*.

Limitations and Obstacles

The project of practical spiritual theology is full of opportunities and possibilities for future development. It also faces some limitations and obstacles. A significant limitation is that the academic literature is full of new approaches and variations on past methods that no one, save the creator of the method, has any familiarity with. This also contributes to the challenge of making practical spiritual theology accessible to the Church. A potential obstacle to the reception of this approach is the tension between doing theology systematically and practically. Spiritual theologians may argue that practical spiritual theology's emphasis on experience could endanger doctrinal truths. Practical theologians may argue that practical spiritual theology's emphasis on the truths of the faith or the teachings of a mystic endangers the primary emphasis on experience.

There is also the obstacle of hermeneutics. There are a few interpretive moves in and around Thomas Groome's model of shared Christian praxis. How can each of these moves be accounted for without doing injustice to the author, text, or readers? In the semi-structured interviews in Southwell, there was the possibility for Hilton to become only an object for associative reasoning, an object for transference for the groups. This could generate misleading understandings of Hilton. While the intention is to form a dialogue and dialectic between the mystic and contemporary Christians, researchers in the present can easily interpret historical mystics in anachronistic ways. Often retrieval efforts by Christians and others involve taking historical practices and persons out of their context in order to read back into them modern concerns.

This is a violation of the integrity of the mystic or the historical practice under consideration. Reformulation of practices for the present must acknowledge the original intention of the practice as best as can be determined from historical evidence. Greater attention needs to be given to these interpretive questions and especially to the formulation of new spiritual theologies that may be the result of a creative synthesis between new and old ideas. There is an improvisational nature to Christian interpretation of the Bible in preaching and other interpretive and hermeneutical endeavors.[23] The method of practical spiritual theology requires similar faithful improvisation when interpreting historical texts and practices for

---

23. Dale Martin, *Pedagogy of the Bible*.

the purposes of the present.[24] This is an area that will benefit from the critical interpretive work of professional theologians and scholars.

CONCLUSION

Walter Hilton refers to the goal of the spiritual life as being "Jerusalem." Jerusalem is a metaphor for the spiritual life and its journey with and toward the Trinity – toward God. This is what the medieval mystic oriented her life toward—union with God. This union cannot be fully realized in this life. For centuries, the mystics and saints have been witnesses to the reality of God. They have been like bonfires on a dark winter's night. They have also been witnesses to human lives rigorously ordered toward God. Practical spiritual theology is a modest effort in comparison to the achievements of these mystics and the venerable shelves of theological libraries about them. Nonetheless, it is a project that intends to draw contemporary Christians into the warmth and light of God's presence by interacting with the writings of these foremothers and forefathers of the faith. These saints of the past can inspire the faith and practice of the saints today. The landscape of today is different from the landscape of yesterday, but it is in so many ways the same journey, with the same wrong turns and the same glorious vistas. In these ways and others, contemporary Christians walk with the mystics of the past toward the same ultimate destination—Jerusalem. Along the way, lives will be changed, communities renewed, and the world blessed.

---

24. While critical academic approaches to interpreting mystical writings can be helpful and are often employed by practical theologians, an ecclesial approach to integrating mystical writings, the approach of spiritual theologians is also essential. For some analogues of these considerations see: Hans Boersma, *Five Things Theologians Wish Biblical Scholars Knew*.

Appendix I
Questions & Exercises

Mystic Bonfires is intended to be a supplementary textbook for a variety of courses in the areas of theology, ministry, and spirituality. This includes advanced undergraduate courses, graduate courses, as well as programs of preparation for various kinds of ministry, whether lay or ordained. For example, programs of preparation for Christian educators and lay ministers.

Instructors may adapt these questions and exercises for the purposes of the courses they are teaching. With some student populations using more than one set of questions or a combination of questions and exercises may be helpful. In all cases, it is recommended that students engage in a project following the practical spiritual theological method.

I. FOR THEOLOGY AND RELIGION STUDENTS

These questions are the most general of the two sets. They require short answers and help students to read the text with greater attention, fostering a general familiarity with the material, especially basic concepts, and definitions.

Appendix I

Chapter I

1) What is mysticism? Have you ever thought of mysticism before? If you have, when and how?

2) What is the name of the theological method presented in this book and what is its purpose?

3) Christians look to the Bible for guidance. What is the relationship between the guidance Christians receive from the Bible and the guidance they receive from mystics?

4) What is spirituality in general and Christian spirituality in particular? If you had to give your own definition of these terms, what would they be?

5) What is spiritual theology?

Questions & Exercises

6) What is practical theology?

7) How do spiritual theology and practical theology differ?

8) The field of Christian Education is sometimes termed Christian Formation. What is the reasoning behind changing the word from education to formation?

9) What are the two traditional pathways of the spiritual life? Briefly describe them.

10) Why should Christians listen to or give attention to the mystics? Give some reasons from the chapter. Do you find these reasons persuasive? Why or why not?

Appendix I

Chapter 2

1) Who was Walter Hilton? Give some of the basic details of his life.

2) What are the titles of the two most influential books that Hilton wrote? Whom were they written for?

3) Why were Hilton's writings so popular in the fourteenth and fifteenth centuries?

4) In traditional Christian monasticism, there is the cenobitic way and the eremitical way. What are the basic definitions of these ways?

5) For Hilton, what was the basic goal and purpose of the spiritual life? What do you think of this goal? How would you define the goal and purpose of the spiritual life?

Questions & Exercises

6) How does Hilton understand the Biblical concept of the Imago Dei?

7) What are the three traditional stages of the mystical life?

8) What is the mixed life according to Hilton?

9) What is the role of grace in Hilton's writings and in practical spiritual theology?

10) Which teaching of Hilton did you find most interesting. Why? Can you see how it would be useful for your own life of faith and that of others?

Appendix I

Chapter 3

1) How can bringing a medieval mystic's ideas into conversation with a contemporary theologian's ideas be helpful?

2) What is the name of Thomas Groome's model presented in the chapter?

3) What are three essential characteristics of Christian education according to Groome? Briefly describe what each characteristic refers to.

4) What is the "Reign of God" according to Groome?

5) What does Groome mean that Christian education and lived Christian faith should have emancipatory ends?

6) What is conation according to Groome?

Questions & Exercises

7) Groome highlights four areas of critical importance to Christian education that are also of critical importance to practical spiritual theology. What are they?

9) What are the steps or movements of Groome's model of "Shared Christian Praxis?"

10) Identify two ideas that caught your interest from the speculative case study involving the research of Nancy Ammerman. Why did they catch your interest? How do you see these ideas relating to your study of theology and religion?

11) What are some of the ideas associated with the concept of a "Mystic Dimension" in Christian education? In your own experience of Christian education, would you say there has been a mystic dimension? If so, why? If not, why?

Appendix I

Chapter 4

1) What is the goal of practical spiritual theology?

2) Where did the author go to conduct research on Hilton and what is the connection between that region and Hilton?

3) What are some of the questions the author used in the interviews? Give specific examples.

4) How did some of the research participants describe or define mysticism? What do you think of their definitions?

5) Why were some of the research participants concerned about individuals who identify themselves as mystics? Do you share those concerns or have different ones?

Questions & Exercises

6) How did some of the research participants respond to the traditional medieval idea of the three states of life? By the traditional definitions, what state of life are you in?

7) How did some of the research participants respond to Hilton's teaching on moderation? Do you agree with their ideas? Why or why not?

8) What are some of the ideas associated with the concept of collective mysticism? Do you see any implications of this concept for theology, religion, and/or the Church?

9) What are some of the ideas associated with the concept of contemplative evangelism? Do you see any implications of this concept for theology, religion, and/or the Church?

10) Does the method of practical spiritual theology only utilize the knowledge of professional theologians? Also, briefly, do you think ordinary Christians should be consulted about theological matters? Why or why not?

Appendix I

Chapter 5

1) What are some possible results of using a practical spiritual theological method?

2) How can stories about saints and mystics be helpful to Christians today? Have you ever been helped by the story of a saint or mystic? If so, how?

3) What are the four major movements of practical spiritual theology? Include in your answer the four steps of movement II.

4) Is practical spiritual theology for formal academic research? If not, what distinguishes the formal and informal use of this method?

5) What were some examples of practical spiritual theology projects and research questions provided by the author? Which one interested you the most? Briefly describe why the question interests you.

Questions & Exercises

6) Identify two ideas from the chapter's discussion of practical spiritual theology as it relates to the Church. What interested you about these ideas? What implications do you see from these ideas for your own study of theology and religion?

7) Identify two ideas from the chapter's discussion of practical spiritual theology as it relates to Society. What interested you about these ideas? What implications do you see from these ideas for your own study of theology and religion?

8) Identify two ideas from the chapter's discussion of practical spiritual theology as it relates to the Academy. What interested you about these ideas? What implications do you see from these ideas for your own study of theology and religion?

9) What are some of the limitations of practical spiritual theology?

10) Generate three research questions for three potential practical spiritual theological projects. These should interest you and relate to your life. Identify the question, the historical mystic, and the intended setting and/or audience of the research.

Appendix I

Exercises

It is recommended that students do at least one of these exercises as a culminating learning activity after reading and discussing the book.

Paper in Practical Spiritual Theology

In this assignment, students will focus on the first two movements of the practical spiritual theological method. I) Select a Mystic and II) Research a Mystic. Students will devote the majority of their paper to the first step of movement II, which is the researching of a mystic's life and ideas, as well as how others have interacted with those ideas. In this sense, it is a research paper.

In a section of their paper, prior to their conclusion, students should outline briefly what contemporary theologian they might have the mystic dialogue with, what group of contemporary Christians they might present and discuss the mystic with, and finally, what new or retrieved Christian practices might be suggested for Christians today as a result of such a process. If a student is preparing for a particular vocation or type of ministry, they should at least briefly relate how what they have learned could impact their future or present work.

For example, a student selects the fourteenth-century German mystic, Meister Eckhart.[1] The student researches his life and times, reads selections of his writings, and what others have said about him. The student then suggests that Eckhart could be brought into conversation with the ideas of the contemporary theologian Christopher David Shaw.[2] The students suggest that the teachings of Eckhart could be presented to a gathering of students on campus. A potential result of this investigation might be greater and more careful attention to the images individuals use for God since Eckhart and Shaw both address the limits of human language to describe transcendent realities. The student is preparing for a career as an academic theologian. The student could relate how careful attention to the limits of language will be an important practice to cultivate in their ongoing studies.

---

1. Colledge and McGinn, *Meister Eckhart: The Essential Sermons Commentaries, Treatises and Defense*.

2. Shaw, *On Mysticism, Ontology, and Modernity*.

Questions & Exercises

Presentation in Practical Spiritual Theology

In this assignment, students follow the same outline for the paper described above, but instead of a formal paper, they deliver a presentation to the class. The presentation, per the instructor's requirements, can be a formal presentation with slides or a more creative presentation incorporating art (e.g., a painting in response to one of Eckhart's sermons), performance (e.g., dressing up as the mystic), or other dynamic elements. Regardless of the style of the presentation, presenters should be prepared after their presentation to respond to questions and comments from the class.

For example, following the same outline in the example above, the student may dress up as Meister Eckhart and have a friend dress up as Christopher David Shaw. The information for the presentation is then delivered as an interview or conversation.

Appendix I

II. FOR THOSE IN TRAINING FOR VARIOUS KINDS OF MINISTRY

These questions and exercises give attention to the practice of ministry and spiritual formation. They will be useful for lay and ordained ministers, spiritual directors, and Christian educators.

Chapter I

1) Explore the notion of theological retrieval.

Let these questions stimulate your response, not limit it. In what ways do you and other Christians regularly benefit from the work of retrieval? In what ways do you engage in the work of retrieval, perhaps unconsciously, even intuitively? How might the work of retrieval relate to your present or future ministry?

2) Respond to the author's metaphor of mystics being like bonfires on a dark winter night.

Let these questions stimulate your response, not limit it. In what ways are the mystics like bonfires? Are "fire" and "warmth" and "light" appropriate theological images for the spiritual life? In what ways might these images and metaphors be helpful and in what ways might they be problematic? How might this metaphor apply to your ministry?

3) Explore notions of ministry silos as it relates to the work of spiritual formation.

Let these questions stimulate your response, not limit it. Do lay and ordained ministers, spiritual directors, and Christian educators share in the same foundational work of spiritual formulation? Is pastoral ministry only

Questions & Exercises

the purview of the ordained? For example, do lay campus ministers do pastoral work? How does this discussion relate to your ministry?

4) Respond to at least two other ideas in the chapter.

Let these prompts stimulate your response, not limit it. What ideas challenged you in the chapter? What ideas confirmed any long-held intuitions of yours? Are there particular fields of study or concepts that relate specifically to your present and future ministry? What new or clarified questions does this chapter raise for you as a Christian and for your ministry?

Chapter Exercise
Define Your Terms

The meaning of terms varies by local ministry setting, confessional tradition, and other factors. Define the meaning of these terms using this book, other course materials, and other resources available to you. You will find many definitions for all of these terms. Give particular attention to how these terms are utilized within your own theological and denominational traditions. You may list more than one definition found from another source but create your own or select one as your "working definition."[3]

---

3. There are definitional resources that can be helpful from a variety of Christian traditions. For example, see Beasely-Topliffe, *The Upper Room Dictionary of Christian Spiritual Formation*. No one resource will be comprehensive enough to reflect the specific usage of all terms in all settings.

Appendix I

Mystic

Spirituality

Christian Spirituality

Theology

Spiritual Theology

Ascetical Theology

Mystical Theology

Spiritual Director

Questions & Exercises

Pastoral Theology

Practical Theology

Christian Education

Spiritual Formation

Discipleship

Saint

Holiness

Sanctification

Appendix I

Chapter 2

1) Response to the broad details of Walter Hilton's life:

Let these questions stimulate your response, not limit it. What is your impression of the time period Hilton lived in? Considering the limited information we have about his background, do you have any impressions about his motivations and experiences? What might have inspired Hilton to move from canon law to become a hermit and from a hermit to become an Augustinian Canon? Can you relate to Hilton in any way?

2) Explore some of the relationships and connections between Hilton's teachings and the Christian doctrines of the Trinity, sin, and salvation.

Let these questions stimulate your response, not limit it. According to Hilton, how has the image of God in human beings been affected by sin? What is the goal of the spiritual life as it relates to the image of God in human beings? How is this goal pursued? Can the goal be fully realized in this life? Is this goal still seen as the primary concern of Christian theologians and leaders today? Do you understand your present and future ministries as being dedicated, at least in part, to addressing these issues as presented by Hilton? Why or why not?

3) Comment on Hilton's guidance to a secular lord considering leaving his familial and business responsibilities to pursue a life of contemplation.

Let these questions stimulate your response, not limit it. Would counsel opposite to what Hilton gave ever be appropriate in a similar situation? Hilton invokes the "law of love" (Romans 13:8-10, James 2:8) as a Biblical warrant for his guidance. Does this application of the law of love seem appropriate to you? Is this law a primary consideration for you in giving guidance or direction to other Christians? What about in discerning your own choices and behaviors? Should love in this sense be foundational to all ministry?

Questions & Exercises

4) Respond to at least two other ideas in the chapter.

Let these prompts stimulate your response, not limit it. What ideas challenge you in the chapter? What ideas confirmed any long-held intuitions of yours? Are there particular teaching or concepts from the chapter that especially relate to your own spiritual life and that of others you know? What new or clarified questions does this chapter raise for you as a Christian and for your practice of ministry?

Chapter Exercise

Live What You Read

Prayerfully review the select teachings of Walter Hilton from this chapter. Choose one teaching to incorporate into your own understanding of the spiritual life and your own practice of that life. Comment on why you selected this teaching and how you envision incorporating it into your everyday life. How might this teaching be helpful in ministering to others and for others?

Appendix I

Chapter 3

1) Respond to Groome's three purposes of Christian Education.

Let these questions stimulate your response, not limit it. How do Groome's three purposes of Christian Education relate to your understanding of Christian Education? Do these purposes compliment your own understanding, conflict with it, or expand it? Practical spiritual theology as a method of retrieval shares these three purposes as it relates to the work of spiritual formation. In your work of formation do you keep these three purposes in mind? What might the work of formation—whether in a church, group, or individual ministry like spiritual direction—look like if it was shaped by these three purposes?

2) How should Christian formational and educational efforts be evaluated?

Let these questions stimulate your response, not limit it. What factors are important to Groome in evaluating Christian education efforts? After preaching a sermon, conducting a spiritual direction session, teaching a class, or some other activity that has formational intent how do you evaluate its effectiveness? Are your criteria for such evaluations similar to Groome's? Can you surmise what criteria Walter Hilton would use in evaluation?

3) Respond to the concept of "conative mysticism."

Let these questions stimulate your response, not limit it. Mystics and mysticism, in general, are sometimes critiqued for being narrowly focused on the self. How does the concept of conative mysticism address this concern? Is mystical experience always an invitation to step away from others in order to step closer to God? Is there value for others in the solitary anchoress' pursuit of God? How might conative mysticism inform your understanding of faith development?

Questions & Exercises

4) Respond to at least two other ideas in the chapter.

Let these prompts stimulate your response, not limit it. What ideas challenge you in the chapter? What ideas would you like to grasp more clearly? Are there particular concepts that relate directly to helpful or less helpful trends you have observed in formation efforts in the Church? What new or clarified questions does this chapter raise for you as a practitioner in your field of ministry? Do the ideas suggest changes to how you practice ministry with, to, and for others?

Chapter Exercise

Dialogue Across the Centuries

Identify at least three historical mystics and three contemporary theologians to be in dialogue with each other. Picture this less as an academic exercise and more of an exercise in the Christian imagination. Picture the mystic and the theologian in actual conversation with each other. Why did you select the conversation partners you did? What intrigues you about the possibilities of these two Christians being in dialogue with each other? Briefly, what potential points of agreement and points of disagreement might arise in each conversation?

Appendix I

Chapter 4

1) Explore the rationale behind the author's use of an open-ended interview with more general questions versus a question-and-answer format looking for specific answers.

Let these questions stimulate your response, not limit it. If the goal of the interviews was to dialogue with participants about Walter Hilton why didn't the author begin with more content about Hilton? Or ask the participants more specific questions about Hilton and his teaching? What might have been the author's motivation in taking a less directive approach? What connections between these issues of research approach can you make with your own work of teaching and facilitating in your specific ministry setting?

2) Respond to participants' characterization of mysticism being otherworldly.

Let these questions stimulate your response, not limit it. How would you define otherworldliness? What would an otherworldly experience be like? How do other participants' responses to the question of mysticism, such as sense of God, nature, and silence, related to the idea of otherworldliness? Is all mysticism expressed in otherworldliness? Is there such a thing as an ordinary mysticism or mysticism that expresses itself in "this worldiness?" When providing guidance to others about the spiritual life how will you describe mysticism to them? Will you counsel them that mysticism is rare and unusual or an ordinary part of the Christian life?

3) Respond to participants' comments about clergy and the contemplative life.

Let these questions stimulate your response, not limit it. The participants, which included lay and ordained participants, were in general agreement that a life of contemplation is largely impossible for clergy today. By extension, this might apply to other Christian workers. Do you agree with the

Questions & Exercises

group's assessment? If it is true that in most cases clergy and active lay ministers cannot pursue the contemplative life (or even the mixed life as envisioned by Hilton) what might this tell us about the Church more broadly? What kind of a Church do you get when it is organized in such a way that few of its leaders are significantly engaged in any form of contemplative living? What might this discussion mean for your own life and ministry?

4) Respond to at least two other ideas in the chapter.

Let these prompts stimulate your response, not limit it. What ideas challenge you in the chapter? What ideas would you like to explore more fully? Are there particular concepts that relate directly to you and your ministry? What new or clarified questions does this chapter raise for you as a Christian seeking God and as a Christian supporting others in their pursuit of God?

Chapter Exercise

Envision a New Teaching

Select one of the tentative spiritual theologies outlined in this chapter. Gather with a small group of other Christians (at least two others) and discuss this teaching and what it might look like if the Church took this teaching seriously and lived it out faithfully in its life. Ideally, you will gather with fellow believers from your own church, small group, or ministry setting. This will enable you to imagine new possibilities in a setting you are all familiar with.

Appendix I

Chapter 5

1) Summarize the purposes and influences on the Practical Spiritual Theological Method.

Let these questions stimulate your response, not limit it. What aspects of practical theology are incorporated into this method? What aspects of spiritual theology are incorporated into this method? What is the purpose of this method? Does it differ from historical study or devotional reading? What are the four movements of this method? Should academic theologians or ministry practitioners use this method?

2) Summarize possible directions and applications of Practical Spiritual Theology.

Let these questions stimulate your response, not limit it. What are the possibilities of practical spiritual theology for your particular field of ministry? For example, for spiritual direction, pastoral ministry, or Christian education. More specifically, what possibilities for a practical spiritual theological method and approach can you envision for your present and future ministry?

3) How can your field of ministry and your own ministry address the three public?

Let these questions stimulate your response, not limit it. How can spiritual formation be a foundation for addressing all three publics? Are there ways you believe the Church has interacted unhelpfully with any of the three publics, how? In what ways? If spiritual formation is about lived Christian faith, should it address concerns of all three publics or only the concerns of the Church? How will you attend to all three publics? Is it desirable that you do so? Do all Christian workers have to give the same attention to all three publics? If not, why not?

Questions & Exercises

4) Respond to at least two other ideas in the chapter.

Let these prompts stimulate your response, not limit it. What ideas challenge you in the chapter? What ideas would you like to explore more fully? Are there particular concepts that relate directly to you and your ministry? What new or clarified questions does this chapter raise for you as a Christian seeking God and as a Christian supporting others in their pursuit of God?

Chapter Exercise

It is recommended that students do at least one of these exercises as a culminating learning experience after reading the book, discussing it with others, and after having completed the previous chapter exercises. Alternatively, students may conduct a research project using the practical spiritual theological method as outlined in the next appendix.

Paper in Practical Spiritual Theology

In this assignment, students will focus on the first two movements of the Practical Spiritual Theological method. I) Select a Mystic and II) Research a Mystic. Students will devote the majority of their paper to the first step of movement II, which is the researching of a mystic's life and ideas, as well as how others have interacted with those ideas. In this sense, it is a research paper.

In a section of their paper, prior to their conclusion, students should outline briefly what contemporary theologian they might have the mystic dialogue with, what group of contemporary Christians they might present and discuss the mystic with (ordinarily this should be the student's present ministry setting), and finally, what new or retrieved Christian practices might be suggested for Christians today (especially those in their ministry setting) as a result of such a process. The student should relate how what they have learned in this project might impact and influence their future ministry.

Appendix I

For example, a student selects the fourteenth-century German mystic, Meister Eckhart. The student researches his life and times, reads selections of his writings, and what others have said about him. The student then suggests that Eckhart could be brought into conversation with the ideas of the contemporary theologian Christopher David Shaw. The students suggest that the teachings of Eckhart could be presented to a gathering of students at their church. A potential result of this investigation might be greater and more careful attention to the images individuals use for God in the church's worship services and public prayers since Eckhart and Christopher David Shaw both address the limits of human language to describe transcendent realities. The student is preparing for a career as an academic theologian. The student could relate how careful attention to the limits of language will be an important practice to cultivate in their ongoing studies.

Presentation in Practical Spiritual Theology

In this assignment, students follow the same outline for the paper described above, but instead of a formal paper, they deliver a presentation to the class. The presentation, per the instructor's requirements, can be a formal presentation with slides or a more creative presentation incorporating art (e.g., a painting in response to one of Eckhart's sermons), performance (e.g., dressing up as the mystic), or other dynamic elements. Regardless of the style of the presentation, presenters should be prepared after their presentation to respond to questions and comments from the class.

For example, following the same outline in the example above, the student may dress up as Meister Eckhart and have a friend dress up as Christopher David Shaw. The information for the presentation is then delivered as an interview or conversation.

Appendix II

Guidelines and Suggestions for Using the Method

The method of practical spiritual theology is flexible. It can be used to guide formal academic research, as well as informal research by faith communities, groups, and individuals.

THE METHOD IN BRIEF

1) Select a Mystic

The method can begin with a specific research question or simply an interest in a mystic and a potential area of inquiry for a specific Christian community. All research questions must fall under the umbrella of how a historical mystic can inspire and resource the faith and practice of Christians today.

2) Research a Mystic

  A. Research and reflection on the mystic.

      a. The mystic's biographical details, writings, and ideas

      b. How others have interacted with the mystic's writings

  This part of the method involves research of primary and secondary sources. It is essentially a literature review. This process will be less extensive in informal practical spiritual theological projects compared to formal academic projects.

B. Research and reflection on a contemporary theologian

    a. The theologian's biographical details, writings, and ideas

    b. A dialogue or mutual analysis of the mystic's and theologians' ideas

    c. Tentative considerations for retrieved, renewed, or reformulated practice

C. Conversation with contemporary Christians

    a. Presentation of mystic's life and ideas

    b. Engagement of ideas by contemporary Christians

    c. Tentative considerations for retrieved, renewed, or reformulated practice

A research question or a general area of inquiry will be needed before beginning step c.

D. Theological reflection toward practice

    a. Prayerfully review steps a-c

    b. Refine tentative considerations for retrieved, renewed, or reformulated practice

3) Suggest New or Renewed Practice

4) Share and Live the Practice

FORMAL ACADEMIC RESEARCH

Those wishing to pursue formal academic research that involves human subjects must secure the permission of and follow the procedures of their university. This will require approval by the institutional review board (IRB) or research ethics committee (REB). It will also require training in academic research and theological reflection methods.

Guidelines and Suggestions for Using the Method

Some faith communities may want to partner, sponsor, or work collaboratively with an academic researcher on a practical spiritual theological project.

INFORMAL PASTORAL RESEARCH

Those conducting informal research will need to give attention to the safety of those participating in the project. Denominational policies regarding the safe gathering of persons should be followed where provided. When in doubt consult the appropriate authorities related to the sponsoring church, institution, or organization.

Faith communities may want to invite an outsider familiar with methods of theological reflection and group facilitation to consult with them about or guide them in their practical spiritual theological project.

IDEAS FOR MYSTIC LABS, INVESTIGATIONS AND PROJECTS

These ideas are suggestive. Their purpose is to inspire creative possibilities for PST projects in faith communities, whether in congregations, small groups, or other settings. These projects will help ministry practitioners and the people of God to be researchers of the Spirit.

The method is flexible, as these ideas will suggest. It is not always necessary to implement the full method, though it is often desirable to do so. These are not complete outlines. They are illustrative in nature.

Mystics Labs for Shorter Projects

Individual Research, Group Presentations

These projects are modest efforts in PST. Nonetheless, they can enrich the faith and practice of Christians today. They can also be the first steps in preparing individuals or communities to engage in longer and more complex PST projects. These projects involve individuals in researching a mystic and then presenting their findings to a group. Here are two potential examples:

Appendix II

A Paper in Practical Spiritual Theology

In this approach, an individual focuses on the first two movements of the practical spiritual theological method. I) Select a Mystic and II) Research a Mystic. The writer will devote the majority of their paper to the first step of movement II, which is the researching of a mystic's life and ideas, as well as how others have interacted with those ideas. In this sense, it is a research paper.

In a section of their paper prior to their conclusion, the writer should outline briefly what contemporary theologian they might have the mystic dialogue with, what group of contemporary Christians they might present and discuss the mystic with (e.g., their local church, ministry settings, etc.), and finally, what new or retrieved Christian practices might be suggested for Christians today as a result of such a process.

For example, an individual selects the fourteenth-century German mystic, Meister Eckhart. The writer researches his life and times, reads selections of his writings, and what others have said about him. The writer then suggests that Eckhart could be brought into conversation with the ideas of the contemporary theologian Christopher David Shaw. The students suggest that the teachings of Eckhart could be presented at a formation class for adults at their church. A potential result of this investigation might be greater and more careful attention to the images individuals use for God since Eckhart and Shaw both address the limits of human language to describe transcendent realities. In some faith communities, this paper could be read, shared, and discussed with others.

A Presentation in Practical Spiritual Theology

In this approach, an individual follows the same outline for the paper described above, but instead of a formal paper, they deliver a presentation to a class, small group, or another gathering. The presentation, as desired by the individual and the expectations of the group, can be a formal presentation with slides or a more creative presentation incorporating art (e.g., a painting in response to one of Eckhart's sermons), performance (e.g., dressing up as the mystic), or other dynamic elements. Regardless of the style of the presentation, presenters should be prepared after their presentation to respond to questions and comments.

Guidelines and Suggestions for Using the Method

For example, following the same outline in the example above, an individual may dress up as Meister Eckhart and have a friend dress up as Shaw. The information for the presentation is then delivered as an interview or conversation.

Either of these approaches could be used helpfully in congregational formation programs. For example, a month on the mystics, with each Sunday featuring a different presentation about a different mystic. This approach could be adapted for children and youth formation as well. For example, Francis of Assisi comes by with some animals. Julian of Norwich speaks to the children from her window while holding a hazelnut. Teresa of Avila speaks to children while holding a castle in her hands. There are many other creative and imaginative possibilities.

Mystic Lab for Longer Projects

Group Theological Reflection Toward Local Practice

It is possible to conduct informal PST projects that do not engage with a contemporary theologian. In these situations, engagement with contemporary ideas happens primarily through engagement with Christians in a particular setting. Here are three potential examples.

Catherine of Siena and Campus Ministry

Research Question: How can the life and writings of Catherine of Siena resource and inspire the social justice work of our campus ministry?

Teresa of Avila and Stewardship of Sacred Places

Research Question: How can St. Teresa's book, *The Interior Castle*, resource and inspire how we steward our historical church building.

Appendix II

The Letters of Catherine of Siena and The Practice of Spiritual Direction

Research Question: How can the letter of St. Catherine resource and inspire our practice of spiritual direction?

In each of these projects, the mystic investigation is driven by a research question for a particular Christian community. In the last example, that community may be a peer supervision group of spiritual directors or a gathering of directors from a particular network or association.

An adapted PST model for these projects could look like the following. The first example, regarding Catherine of Siena and a campus ministry's social justice work, will be used as an example.

I) Select a Mystic:

In this example, the fourteenth-century Italian mystic, Catherine of Siena has been chosen. Two leaders in the campus ministry know something about Catherine of Siena and her life of social witness. For several weeks the leadership of the campus ministry has felt that their social justice efforts lack a substantial spiritual grounding. Catherine is seen as a possible resource to address this challenge.

   A. Research a Mystic

      a. Research and reflection on the mystic.

      b. The mystic's biographical details, writings, and idea

      c. How others have interacted with the mystic's writings

This research can be done by a core group or shared across the community.

In this hypothetical example, the campus ministry staff members, board members, and key volunteers do some preliminary reading on Catherine. However, they want to involve the entire community in the process of becoming familiar with Catherine's life, writings, and ideas. To facilitate this wider engagement they invite the entire campus ministry community to read certain materials about Catherine of Siena. They also provide opportunities for discussion of these materials over a period of a month.

Guidelines and Suggestions for Using the Method

2) Conversation with contemporary Christians

    a. Presentation of mystic's life and ideas

    b. Engagement of ideas by Contemporary Christians

    c. Tentative considerations for retrieved, renewed, or reformulated practice

The project could move forward in a linear fashion by holding off any discussions of how Catherine might inspire and resource their social justice work until the initial study period by the community is over. Then a final culminating session could be had where the community is invited to reflect on all they have learned about Catherine of Siena and relate it to their social justice work.

This can be done more informally and intuitively through brainstorming and open-ended conversations. It can also be done more formally with the help of a skilled facilitator guiding the community in reflecting on Catherine and in reflecting on their current practice of social justice.

There are many resources on leading group discussions and reflections that can help the PST process. This is where the skills of a consultant or academic researcher can be invaluable. However, with patience, preparation, and practice, many PST projects can be facilitated and guided from within a community.

It might also be possible to combine the research and conversation phases in the campus ministry example. This would mean telling the community from the start about the research question and keeping the research question forefront in people's minds as they read and discuss the materials about Catherine of Siena. Whether done in tandem or as separate steps, the process should result in some tentative consideration for future practice.

1) Theological reflection toward practice

    a. Prayerfully review steps a-c

    b. Refine tentative considerations for retrieved, renewed, or reformulated practice

Appendix II

The core group then collects all the reflections and ideas shared from all previous sessions. They identify potential aspects of Catherine's spirituality and practice that can be retrieved, renewed, or reformulated for their social justice work.

1) Suggest New or Renewed Practice

These new or renewed practices are then suggested or presented to the campus ministry's leadership before they are recommended to the wider campus ministry community. This movement could have several more steps before the community determines what the new practices and approach will be. These additional steps might include listening sessions and surveys of the wider campus community.

2) Share and Live the Practice

The core group shares the results of their theological investigations and reflections. This sharing is first to their own community as outlined in the previous movement. Sharing to other groups may follow, such as other campus ministries in their denominational or ecumenical networks. Sharing the results of a PST project may be done through a formal report, a visual presentation, video, or a combination of these and other approaches. This entire project could take anywhere from a few weeks to a couple of months to complete. PST projects done in smaller group settings with more modest goals could be completed in less time. Perhaps as short as a month from the conception of the project to its completion. The same project idea could be expanded to include the full PST method. In this case, adding the movement and steps associated with including the ideas of a contemporary theologian.

Mystic Labs: Extended Projects

Initiatives in Transformation

The possibilities for extended, long-term, PST projects were mentioned in chapter four. More reflection and research will be needed in order to be able to outline how such projects may be conceptualized and implemented. An example of a long-term project given in chapter four is the ongoing

Guidelines and Suggestions for Using the Method

work of raising awareness about and engagement with Walter Hilton by contemporary Christians. This project has a local and global focus. The local focus being the historic places associated with Walter Hilton, such as Thurgarton and Southwell in England. This extended project may involve creating accessible resources about Walter Hilton, presentations about Walter Hilton, commissioning an icon of Walter Hilton, events and resources for observing Walter Hilton's feast day, as well as additional PST projects about Walter Hilton, both academic and informal. Long-term PST projects may be characterized by a number of initiatives.

Bibliography

Allen, Diogenes. *Spiritual Theology: The Theology of Yesterday for Spiritual Help Today.* Lanham, MD: Cowley, 1997.
Allen, Joseph. *The Ministry of the Church: Image of Pastoral Care.* New York: St. Vladimir's Seminary Press, 1986
Allen, Rosamund. *Richard Rolle: The English* Writings. New York: Paulist, 1988.
Allmand, Christopher. *The Hundred Years War.* Cambridge: Cambridge University Press, 1988.
Ammerman, Nancy, ed. *Everyday Religion: Observing Modern Religious Lives.* Oxford: Oxford University Press, 2007.
———, et al. *Studying Congregations: A New Handbook.* Nashville: Abingdon Press, 1998.
———. *Sacred Stories, Spiritual Tribes: Finding Religion in Everyday Life.* Oxford: Oxford University Press, 2014.
Andrews, Alan, ed. *The Kingdom Life: A Practical Theology of Discipleship and Spiritual Formation.* Colorado Springs: NavPress, 2010.
Anthony, Michael, ed. *Christian Education: Foundations for the Twenty-first Century.* Grand Rapids: Baker, 2001.
Aquinas, Thomas. *Summa Theologiae.* 5 vols. Notre Dame: Christian Classics, 1948.
Astley, Jeff. *Ordinary Theology: Looking, Listening, and Learning in* Theology. Surrey, UK: Ashgate, 2002.
Augustine. *Confessions.* Translated by Henry Chadwick. New York: Oxford University Press, 2009.
Aumann, Jordan. *Spiritual Theology.* New York: Bloomsbury, 2018.
Avila, Teresa. *The Interior Castle.* Gastonia, NC: Tan Books, 2011.
Bakke, Jeannette. *Holy Invitations: Exploring Spiritual Direction.* Grand Rapids: Baker, 2000.
Ball, Peter. *Anglican Spiritual Direction.* New York: Church Publishing, 2007.
Balswick, Jack, et al. *The Reciprocating Self: Human Development in Theological Perspective.* Downers Grove, IL: IVP, 2005.
Barker, Juliet. *1381: The Year of the Peasants' Revolt.* Cambridge, MA: Harvard University Press, 2014.
Barton, Ruth Haley. *Invitation to Solitude and Silence: Experiencing God's Transforming Presence.* Downers Grove: IVP, 2010.
Beasely-Topliffe, K., ed. *The Upper Room Dictionary of Christian Spiritual Formation.* Nashville: Upper Room, 2003.
Beeson, Trevor. *The Deans.* London: SCM, 2004.

Bibliography

Bernard, McGinn. *The Varieties of Vernacular Mysticism: 1350-1550*. New York: Crossroad, 2012.

Blythe, Teresa A. *50 Ways to Pray: Practices from Many Traditions and Times*. Nashville, Abingdon Press, 2006.

Boersma, Hans. *Five Things Theologians Wish Biblical Scholars Knew*. Downers Grove: IVP, 2021.

Boff, Clodovis. *Theology and Praxis: Epistemological Foundations*: Eugene, OR: Wipf and Stock, 1987.

The Book of Common Prayer. New York: Church Publishing, 1977.

Bourdieu, Pierre. *Outline of a Theory of Practice*. Translated by Richard Nice. Cambridge: Cambridge University Press, 2013.

Bradshaw, Paul, and John Melloh. *Foundations in Ritual Studies*. Grand Rapids: Baker Academic, 2007.

The British Pilgrimage Trust. "Southwell Minster Pilgrimage in a Day." https://britishpilgrimage.org/portfolio/southwell-minster-pilgrimage-in-a-day/

Brother Lawrence of the Resurrection. *The Practice of the Presence of God*. Translated by Salvatore Sciburba. Washington, DC: ICS, 1994.

Browning, Don. *A Fundamental Practical Theology*. Minneapolis: Fortress, 1996.

Burrows, Ruth. *Guidelines for Mystical Prayer*. Denville, NJ: Dimension Books, 1980.

Buschart, David, and Kent Eilers. *Theology as Retrieval: Receiving the Past, Renewing the Church*. Downers Grove, IL: InterVarsity Academic, 2015.

Bushofsky, Dennis, Richard W. Rouse, and Suzanne Burke, eds. *Go Make Disciples: An Invitation to Baptismal Living: A Handbook to the Catechumenate*. Minneapolis: Augsburg, 2012.

Cahalan, Kathleen, and Gordon Mikoski, eds. *Opening the Field of Practical Theology: An Introduction*. Lanham, Maryland: Roward & Littlefield, 2014.

Cameron, Helen, et al. *Studying Local Churches: A Handbook*. London: SCM, 2005.

Catherine of Siena. *The Dialogue*. Edited by Suzanne Noffke. New York: Paulist, 1980.

Cavallini, Giuliana. *Catherine of Siena*. New York: Geoffrey Chapman, 1998.

Chan, Simon. *Spiritual Theology: A Systematic Study of the Christian Life*. Downers Grove, IL: IVP, 1998.

Chandler, Diane. *Christian Spiritual Formation: An Integrated Approach for Personal and Relational Wholeness*. Downers Grove, IL: IVP, 2014.

Chaucer, Geoffrey. Translated by Peter G. Beidler. *The Canterbury Tales*. New York: Bantam, 2006.

Clark, John, and Rosemary Dorward, eds. *Walter Hilton: The Scale of Perfection*. New York: Paulist, 1991.

Clarke, Peter, and Sarah James, eds. *Pastoral Care in Medieval England: Interdisciplinary Approaches*. New York: Routledge, 2020.

Clebsh, William, and Charles Jaekle, eds. *Pastoral Care in Historical Perspective*. Northvale, NJ: Jason Aroson, Inc, 1994.

Clement, Olivier. *The Roots of Christian Mysticism: Texts from the Patristic Era with Commentary*. New York: New City, 1993.

Colledge, Edmond, and Bernard McGinn, trans. *Meister Eckhart: The Essential Sermons Commentaries, Treatises and Defense: Classics of Western Spirituality Series*. Mahwah: NJ, Paulist Press, 1981.

College, Eric, ed. *The Mediaeval Mystics of England*. New York: Charles Scribner's Sons, 1961.

Bibliography

Copeland, M. Shawn. *Enfleshing Freedom: Body, Race, and Being*. Minneapolis, Fortress, 2010.

Creswell, John. *Research Design: Qualitative, Quantitative, and Mixed Methods Approaches*. Los Angeles: Sage, 2014.

Cummings, Charles. *Monastic Practices*. Kalamazoo, MI: Cistercian Publications, 1986.

Dales, Douglas, ed. *Glory Descending: The Spiritual Theology of Michael Ramsey*. Grand Rapids: Eerdmans, 2005.

Davies, Oliver. *God Within: The Mystical Tradition of Northern Europe*. New York: New City, 2006.

Davis, Carmel. *Mysticism & Space: Space and Spatiality in the Works of Richard Rolle, The Cloud of Unknowing and Julian of Norwich*. Washington, D.C.: The Catholic University of America, 2008.

Dawn, Marva, and Peterson, Eugene. *The Unnecessary Pastor: Rediscovering the Call*. New York: Eerdmans, 1999.

Demacopoulos, George. *Five Models of Spiritual Direction in the Early Church*. Notre Dame, IN: University of Notre Dame Press, 2007.

Dreher, Rod. *The Benedict Option: A Strategy for Christians in a Post-Christian Nation*. New York: Penguin Random House, 2017.

Dreyer, Elizabeth, and Mark Burrows, eds. *Minding the Spirit: The Study of Christian Spirituality*. Baltimore: John Hopkins University Press, 2005.

Edwards, Tilden. *Spiritual Director, Spiritual Companion: Guide to Tending the Soul*. New York: Paulist, 2001.

Episcopal Church. *Lesser Feasts and Fasts*. New York: Church Publishing, 2019.

Fagerberg, David. *Liturgical Mysticism*. Steubenville, OH: Emmaus Academic, 2019.

Fanous, Samuel, and Vincent Gillespie, ed. *The Cambridge Companion to Medieval English Mysticism*. Cambridge: Cambridge University Press, 2011.

Farley, Edward. *Theologia: The Fragmentation and Unity of Theological Education*. Eugene, OR: Wipf and Stock, 2001.

Forest, Jim. *Praying with Icons*. New York: Orbis, 2008.

Fox, Matthew. *Julian of Norwich: Wisdom in a Time of Pandemic and Beyond*. Bloomington: iUniverse, 2020.

Frei, Hans. *The Eclipse of Biblical Narrative: A Study in Eighteenth and Nineteenth Century Hermeneutics*. New Haven, CT: Yale University Press, 1974.

Freire, Paulo. *Pedagogy of the Oppressed*. New York: Seabury, 1970.

Fry, Timothy, Timothy Horner, and Imogene Baker, eds. *The Rule of St. Benedict*. Collegeville: Liturgical, 1981.

Gatta, Julia. *Life in Christ: Practicing Christian Spirituality*. New York: Church Publishing, 2018.

Gatta, Julia. *Three Spiritual Directors for Our Time*. Cambridge: Cowley, 1986.

Gerben, Heitnik. *Practical Theology: History, Theory, Action Domains*. Grand Rapids: Eerdmans, 1993.

Goergen, Donald J. *St. Dominic: The Story of a Preaching Friar*. Paulist Press, 2016.

Graham, Elaine. *Between a Rock and a Hard Place: Public Theology in a Post-Secular Age*. London: SCM, 2013.

———. *Transforming Practice: Pastoral Theology in an Age of Uncertainty*. Eugene, OR: Wipf and Stock, 1996.

Greer, Rowan. *Anglican Approaches to Scripture: From the Reformation to the Present*. New York: Crossroads, 2006.

Bibliography

Grenz, Stanley J., and Roger Olson. *Who Needs Theology: An Invitation to the Study of God*. Downers Grove, IL: IVP, 1996.

Griffen, Emilie, ed. *Hildegard of Bingen: Selections from Her Writings*. Translated by Columba Hart and Jane Bishop. New York: HarperOne, 2005.

Groome, Thomas. *Sharing Faith: A Comprehensive Approach to Religious Education and Pastoral Ministry: The Way of Shared Praxis*. Eugene, OR: Wipf and Stock, 1991.

Gutierrez, Gustavo. *A Theology of Liberation*. New York: Orbis, 1988.

Harris, Maria. *Fashion Me a People: Curriculum in the Church*. Louisville: Westminster John Knox, 1989.

Harrison, Tish Warren. *Liturgy of the Ordinary*. Downers Grove, IVP, 2019.

Hatcher, John. *The Black Death*. Philadelphia: Da Capo, 2008.

Heath, Elaine. *The Mystic Way of Evangelism: A Contemplative Vision for Christian Outreach*. Grand Rapids: Baker Academic, 2008.

Hess, Carol Lakey. "Religious Education." In *The Wiley-Blackwell Companion to Practical Theology*, 299–307. Malden, MA: Blackwell, 2012.

Hiestand, Gerald, and Todd Wilson. *The Pastor Theologian: Resurrecting an Ancient Vision*. Grand Rapids: Zondervan, 2015.

Hill, Andrew, and John Walton, eds. *A Survey of the Old Testament*. 3rd ed. Grand Rapids: Zondervan, 2009.

Hillman, Jennifer, and Tingle, Elizabeth, eds. *Soul Travel: Spiritual Journeys in Late Medieval and Early Modern Europe*. Oxford: Peter Lang International Academic Publishers, 2019.

Hiltner, Seward. *Preface to Pastoral Theology*. Nashville: Abingdon, 1958.

Hilton, Walter. *8 Chapters on Perfection & Angel's Song*. Translated by Rosemary Dorward. Oxford: SLG, 1992.

Hirsch, Alan. *The Forgotten Ways*. Grand Rapids: Brazos, 2006.

Horobin, Simon, and Linner R. Mooney, eds. *Middle English Texts in Translation*. Suffolk, UK: York Medieval, 2014.

Isasi-Diaz, Ada Maria, and Eduardo Mendieta, eds. *Decolonizing Epistemologies: Latina/o Theology and Philosophy*. New York: Fordham University Press, 2012.

James, William. *The Varieties of Religious Experience*. New York: The Library of America, 1987.

James, William. *Varieties of Religious Experience*. New York: Library of America, 1987.

Jeffery, David, ed. *Toward a Perfect Love: The Spiritual Counsel of Walter Hilton*. Vancouver: Regent College Publishing, 1985.

Johnson, Eric, ed. *Psychology & Christianity: Five Views*. Downers Grove, IL: Interrvarsity, 2010.

———. *Foundations for Soul Care: A Christian Psychology Proposal*. Downers Grove, IL: IVP, 2007.

Jones, E.A., ed. *The Medieval Mystical Tradition in England*. Woodbridge, Suffolk: D.S. Brewer, 2013.

Julian of Norwich. *Julian of Norwich: Showings*. Edited by James Walsh. Mahwah: Paulist, 1978.

Keating, James, ed. *Spirituality and Moral Theology: Essays from a Pastoral Perspective*. New York: Paulist, 2000.

Kempe, Margery. *The Book of Margery Kempe*. London: Penguin, 2019.

Kerchberger, Claire. *Walter Hilton: The Goad of Love*. Whitefish: Kessinger, 2013.

Bibliography

Kershaw, Simon. *Exciting Holiness. Collects and Readings for the Festivals and Lesser Festivals of the Calendar of the Church of the Church of England, the Church of Ireland, the Scottish Episcopal Church and The Church in Wales.* Norwich, UK: Canterbury Press, 2007.

Knox, John. *Foxe's Book of Martyrs.* Mt. Sterling, KY: Reformation Publishers, 2010.

Laferriere, Anik. "The Austin Friars in Pre-Reformation England." Ph.D. diss. University of Oxford, 2017.

Lamm, Julia, ed. *The Widely Blackwell Companion to Christian Mysticism.* Hoboken: Blackwell, 2017.

———, ed., *Christian Mysticism.* Hoboken: Wiley Blackwell.

Leech, Kenneth. *Experiencing God: Theology as Spirituality.* Eugene, OR: Wipf and Stock, 1985.

Levy, Ian Christopher. *Introducing Medieval Biblical Interpretation: The Senses of Scripture in Premodern Exegesis.* Grand Rapids: Baker Academic, 2018.

Liebert, Elizabeth. *The Art of Discernment: Spiritual Practices for Decision Making.* Louisville, Westminster, 2008.

Lindbeck, George. *The Nature of Doctrine: Religion and Theology in a Postliberal Age.* 25th Anniversary Edition. Louisville, Westminster, 2009.

Luongo, F. Thomas. *The Saintly Politics of Catherine of Siena.* Ithaca: Cornell University Press, 2006.

———. *The Saint Politics of Catherine of Siena.* Ithaca: Cornell University Press, 2006.

Martin, Dale. *Pedagogy of the Bible. An Analysis and Proposal.* Louisville: Westminster John Knox, 2008.

Mattewes-Green, Frederica. *The Jesus Prayer: The Ancient Desert Prayer that Tunes the Heart to God.* Brewster, MA: Paraclete, 2009.

Mayhew-Smith, Nick. *The Naked Hermit: A Journey to The Heart of Celtic Britain.* London: SPK, 2019.

McGinn, Bernard. *The Flowering of Mysticism: Men and Women in the New Mysticism, 1200-1350.* New York: Crossroad, 1998.

McGrath, Alister. *Christian Spirituality: An Introduction.* Oxford: Blackwell Publishing, 2003.

McMinn, Mark, and Timothy Phillips, eds. *Care for the Soul: Exploring the Intersection of Psychology and Theology.* Downers Grove, IL: IVP, 2001.

McMinn, Mark. *Psychology, Theology, and Spirituality.* Carol Stream, IL: Tyndale House, 1996.

Mercer, Joyce Ann. "Feminist and Womanist Practical Theology." In *Opening the Field of Practical Theology: An Introduction*, edited by Kathleen A. Cahalan and Gordon S. Mikoski, 97–114. Lanham: Rowman & Littlefield, 2014.

Merton, Thomas. *Emblems of a Season of Fury.* New York: New Directions, 1963.

Milbank, John. *Theology and Social Theory: Beyond Secular Reason.* Malden: Blackwell, 2006.

Miller-McLemore, Bonnie J. *The Wiley-Blackwell Companion to Practical Theology.* Malden, MA: Blackwell, 2012.

Mortimer, Ian. *The Time Traveler's Guide to Medieval England.* New York: Simon & Schuster, 2008.

Moules, Nancy J., et al. *Conducting Hermeneutic Research: From Philosophy to Practice.* New York: Peter Lang, 2015.

Nassif, Bradley, et al. *Christian Spirituality: Four Views.* Grand Rapids: Zondervan, 2012.

Bibliography

Niebuhr, Richard, H., *The Meaning of Revelation*. Louisville: Westminister, 2006.

Noffke, Suzanne. *Catherine of Siena: Vision through a Distant Eye*. New York: Authors Choice, 2006.

Nouwen, Henri. *The Way of the Heart: Connecting with God Through Prayer, Wisdom, and Silence*. New York: Ballantine Books, 1981.

O'Reilley, Mary Rose. *Radical Presence: Teaching as Contemplative Practice*. Portsmouth, NH: Boynton/Cook, 1998.

Ottati, Douglas F. Introduction to *The Meaning of Revelation*, by H. Richard Niebuhr, ix– xxxii. Louisville: Westminster, 2006.

Otto, Rudolph. *The Idea of the Holy: An Inquiry into the Non-Rational Factor in the Idea of the Divine and its Relation to the Rational*. Oxford: Oxford University Press, 1952.

Palmer, Parker. *A Hidden Wholeness: The Journey Toward an Undivided Life*. Hoboken: Jossey-Bass, 2009.

———. *To Know As We Are Known: Education As a Spiritual Journey*. New York: Harper Collins, 1993.

———. *To Know As We Are Known: Education As a Spiritual Journey*. New York: Harper Collins, 1993.

Pantin, W.A. *The English Church in the Fourteenth Century*. Toronto: Toronto University Press, 1980.

Peacock, Barbara. *Soul Care in African American Practice*. Downers Grove, IL, 2020.

Pecknold, C. C.. "The Dominican Option. First Things. October 6, 2014. https://www.firstthings.com/web-exclusives/2014/10/the-dominican-option

Peters, Greg. *The Monkhood of All Believers: The Monastic Foundation of Christian Spirituality*. Grand Rapids: Baker Academic, 2018.

Peters, Greg. *The Story of Monasticism: Retrieving an Ancient Tradition for Contemporary Spirituality*. Grand Rapids: Baker Academic, 2015.

Plantinga, Harry, ed. *Walter Hilton: Treatise Written to a Devout Man*. Aeterna, 2015.

Purves, Andrew. *Pastoral Theology in the Classical Tradition*. Louisville: Westminster, 2001.

———. *Reconstructing Pastoral Theology: A Christological Foundation*. Louisville: Westminster John Knox, 2004.

Rahner, Karl. *Karl Rahner: Theologian of the Graced Searched for Meeting*. Edited by Geffrey B. Kelly. St. Paul: Fortress Press, 1992.

Raitt, Jill, ed. *Christian Spirituality: High Middle Ages and Reformation*. New York: Crossroad, 1989.

Rendle, Gil, and Alice Mann. *Holy Conversations: Strategic Planning as Spiritual Practice for Congregations*. Lanham: Rowan & Littlefield, 2003.

Rennie, Kriston. *Medieval Canon Law*. Croydon: UK, Arc Humanities, 2018.

Richard Foster. *Streams of Living Water: Celebrating the Great Traditions of Christian Faith*. New York: Harper Collins, 1998.

Ricoeur, Paul. *Hermeneutics & The Human Sciences*. Cambridge, MA: Cambridge Press, 1981.

Riehle, Wolfgang. *The Secret Within: Hermits, Recluses, and Spiritual Outsiders in Medieval England*. Ithaca: Cornell University Press, 2014.

Rolf, Veronica Mary. *Julian's Gospel: Illuminating the Life & Revelations of Julian of Norwich*. New York: Orbis, 2013.

Root, Andrew. *Faith Formation in a Secular Age*. Grand Rapids: Baker Academic, 2017.

Bibliography

Ross, Susan. *Extravagant Affections. A Feminist Sacramental Theology.* New York: Continuum, 2001.

Savage, Anne, and Nicholas Watson, trans. *Anchoritic Spirituality: Ancrene Wisse and Associated Works.* Paulist, 1991.

Scharen, Christian. *Fieldwork in Theology: Exploring the Social Context of God's Work in the World.* Grand Rapids: Baker Academic, 2015.

Schleiermacher, Friedrich. *Brief Outline of Theology as a Field of Study.* 3rd ed. Translated by Terrence N. Tice. Louisville: John Knox, 2011.

Schreiter, Robert. *Constructing Local Theologies.* Maryknoll: Orbis Books, 1985.

Shaw, Christopher David. *On Mysticism, Ontology, and Modernity: A Theological Engagement with Secularity.* Oxford: Peter Lang, 2018.

Shaw, Jane. "The Potential of Cathedrals." Anglican Theological Review 95, no. 1 (Winter 2013): 137–147.

Smith, David, and Felch, Susan M., eds. *Teaching and Christian Imagination.* Grand Rapids: Eerdmans, 2016.

Sobrino, John. *Spirituality of Liberation: Toward Political Holiness.* Translated by Robert R. Barr. New York: Maryknoll, 1998.

Standish, N. Graham. *Becoming a Blessed Church: Forming a Church of Spiritual Purpose, Presence, and Power.* Hendon: VR: Alban Institute, 2005.

Swinton, John and Mowat, Harriet. *Practical Theology and Qualitative Research.* London: SCM, 2016.

Thornton, Martin. *Christian Proficiency.* Eugene, OR: Wipf and Stock, 1988.

———. *English Spirituality: An Outline of Ascetical Theology According to the English Pastoral Tradition.* Eugene, OR: Wipf and Stock, 1986.

Thurston, Herbert, and Donald Attwater. eds. *Butler's Lives of the Saints.* London: Burns & Oates, 1956.

Tickle, Phyllis. *The Divine Hours Volumes One, Two, Three.* New York: Doubleday, 2006.

Tillich, Paul. *The Essential Tillich: An Introduction to the Writings of Paul Tillich.* Chicago: University of Chicago Press, 1999.

Tracy, David. *Blessed Rage for Order: The New Pluralism in Theology.* Chicago: Harper Collins, 1996.

———. *The Analogical Imagination: Christian Theology and the Culture of Pluralism.* New York: Crossroad, 2013.

Tweed, Thomas. *Crossing and Dwelling: A Theory of Religion.* Cambridge, MA: Harvard University Press, 2006. Kindle.

Underhill, Evelyn. *The Mystics of the Church.* New York: Aeterna, 2015.

Ursula, King. *Christian Mystics: Their Lives and Legacies throughout the Ages.* New York: Simon and Schuster, 1998.

Van Bavel, Tarsicus, trans. *The Rule of St. Augustine.* New York: Doubleday, 1986.

van der Ven, Johannes. *Ecclesiology in Context.* Grand Rapids: Eerdmans, 1993.

———. *Practical Theology: An Empirical Approach.* Leuven, Belgium: Peeters, 1998.

Vatican Council II. *Lumen Gentium.* In *Vatican Council II: The Conciliar and Post Conciliar Documents.* Edited by Austin Flannery. New York: Costello, 1975.

Volf, Miroslav. *A Public Faith: How Followers of Christ Should Serve the Common Good.* Grand Rapids: Brazos, 2011.

Walford, Stephen. *Communion of Saints: The Unity of Divine Love in the Mystical Body of Christ.* Brooklyn: Angelico, 2016.

Walsh, James, ed. *Pre-Reformation English Spirituality.* London: Burns & Oates, 1966.

Bibliography

———, ed. *The Cloud of Unknowing*. Mahwah: Paulist, 1981.
Walshe, Maurice O'C., trans. *The Complete Mystical Works of Meister Eckhart*. New York: Crossroad, 1987. 83–90.
Webster, John. "Theologies of Retrieval." In *The Oxford Handbook of Systematic Theology*, edited by John Webster, Kathryn Tanner, and Iain Torrance, 583–599. Oxford: Oxford University Press, 2008.
Westerhoff, John. *Will Our Children Have Faith?* Harrisburg, PA: Morehouse Publishing, 2012.
White, James. *The Rise of the Nones*. Ada, MI: Baker, 2014.
Williams, Rowan. *Faith in the Public Square*. London: Bloomsbury, 2012.
Wolterstorff, Nicholas. *The Mighty and the Almighty: An Essay in Political Theology*. Cambridge: Cambridge University Press, 2012.
Woods, Richard. *Mysticism and Prophecy: The Dominican Tradition*. Orbis, 1998.
Wright, N.T. *Jesus and the Victory of God*. Minneapolis: Fortress, 1996.
Yarhouse, Mark, et al. *Modern Psychopathologies: A Comprehensive Christian Appraisal*. Downers, Grove IL: IVP, 2005.
Yolf, Miroslav. *A Public Faith: How Followers of Christ Should Serve the Common Good*. Grand Rapids: Brazos, 2011.

www.ingramcontent.com/pod-product-compliance
Lightning Source LLC
Chambersburg PA
CBHW070910160426
43193CB00011B/1419